LEADERS OF RELIGION

General Editor
Reverend Professor C. W. Dugmore, D.D.

Richard Baxter

Richd Baxter.

1615. — 1691.

RICHARD BAXTER *by an unknown artist*
Dr Williams's Library

Richard Baxter

GEOFFREY F. NUTTALL

NELSON

THOMAS NELSON AND SONS LTD
36 Park Street London W1
Parkside Works Edinburgh 9
P.O. Box 336 Apapa Lagos
P.O. Box 25012 Nairobi

THOMAS NELSON (AUSTRALIA) LTD
597 Little Collins Street Melbourne

THOMAS NELSON & SONS (SOUTH AFRICA) (PROPRIETARY) LTD
P.O. Box 9881 Johannesburg

THOMAS NELSON AND SONS (CANADA) LTD
81 Curlew Drive Don Mills Ontario

THOMAS NELSON AND SONS
Copewood and Davis Streets Camden 3, N.J.

———

First published 1965

© Geoffrey F. Nuttall 1965

Printed in Great Britain by
Thomas Nelson (Printers) Ltd, London and Edinburgh

Contents

Foreword

THE claim of Richard Baxter (1615–91) to a place among Leaders of Religion in Britain is not likely to be questioned. During the period of revolution in religion and politics through which he lived he was in touch with many of the most notable figures on both sides of the great divide. At a number of points he also himself contributed to the course of events. His pastoral ideals and achievements as Vicar of Kidderminster, his concern for Christian unity both locally and more widely, his passionately devotional spirit, his honest endeavours to resolve all manner of problems of mind and conscience found expression in a considerable correspondence, in a stream of publications and in a movement for associations of ministers throughout the country; and during the Commonwealth and Protectorate his reputation grew steadily. The Restoration of 1660 brought a complete reversal. Henceforward his lot was exclusion and opposition. Yet in his dignified acceptance of frustration for Christ's sake, in his unbroken eagerness for comprehension and a large measure of tolerance and in his indefatigable writing the stature of the man became more evident. In the century after his death men looked back to him as a founding-father not only of nonconformity but of both the rationalising and the evangelical movements in the Church. His devotional books also continued to shape the piety of many a home. In our own day a succession of studies still draws attention to the fascination of his many-sided personality.

Baxter's own long posthumous autobiography inevitably provides the groundwork for any consideration of his life and lifework. In the following pages this has been filled out, and at times corrected, both from innumerable references to his life and times scattered through his other published works and from his manuscript correspondence, which the present writer has calendared and is the first to have read in chronological order.

Although this is a short book, it is the outcome of more than twenty years' intensive study of its subject. I am grateful for help and encouragement from very many over so long a period. I hope it will not be invidious to mention four names. The late Dr F. J. Powicke, whose two-volume *Life* forms the last critical biography of Baxter, first invited me to read Baxter, indeed urged me so solemnly that I could not but feel he looked on me as his Elisha. The late A. G. Matthews followed my work with constant and friendly support. For thirty years his biographical register of the ministers ejected from their livings in 1660–2, too modestly entitled *Calamy Revised*, has been more often in my hands than almost any other book. Dr Williams's Librarian (the Rev. Roger Thomas) and his staff have been unfailingly helpful in providing me with access to Baxter's works and to the mass of his manuscripts, a large part of which Mr Thomas has elucidated in *Baxter Treatises*. His reading and commenting on the typescript of this book is only one of the invariable kindnesses shown me by Mr Thomas through many years. Mr Anthony Spalding has discussed the book with me at all its stages, especially with reference to its presentation and proportions; and in the tedious work of correcting the proof sheets and compiling the index he has given help of a kind which one can ask only from a true friend.

Finally, I must thank Dr Williams's Trustees for permission to reproduce as the frontispiece the portrait of Richard Baxter which adorns their Library.

G. F. N.

Summer, 1965

Note on Abbreviations

REFERENCES to Baxter's published works, which unless stated otherwise are to first editions, are by an italicised number, which is the number of the work cited as printed in the list of Baxter's works in the appendix, followed, if necessary, by number of part or pagination, and by page-number. To this there is one exception: references to *Reliquiae Baxterianae* are by the abbreviation *R.B.*, followed by number of volume, part and section, and, if necessary, paragraph. Spelling as printed has been reproduced.

References to Baxter's manuscript correspondence are by the number of the volume, followed by the number of the folio on which the letter begins. Spelling has been modernised.

The following abbreviations have been used:

D.W.L. MS(s).: Dr Williams's Library, Baxter Manuscript(s).

Powicke, i: F. J. Powicke, *Life of the Reverend Richard Baxter 1615–1691*, 1924.

Powicke, ii: F. J. Powicke, *The Reverend Richard Baxter under the Cross (1662–1691)*, 1927.

R.B.: *Reliquiae Baxterianae*, edited by M. Sylvester, 1696.

Swarthmore MSS.: Swarthmore Manuscripts, Library of the Society of Friends, Friends House, Euston Road, London N.W.1.

The Salopian

'When I was young (yea till 20 years of age) I durst not have gone into a dark room alone; or if I had, the fear of it would have made me even tremble.'[1]

'I never awaked since I had the use of memory, but I found my self coming out of a dream.'[2]

'. . . the case as I remember when I was a boy our School was in, when we had barred out our Master: . . . when we had got out our Master and shut fast the doors, we grew bold, and talkt to him at our pleasure; then no one was Master, and every one was Master: we spend our time in playing and quarelling . . .'[3]

'When I was young, I was wont to go up the Wrekin Hill with great pleasure (being near my dwelling) and to look down on the Country below me, and see the Villages as little things: . . .'[4]

RICHARD BAXTER was born on Sunday, 12 November 1615, at the village of Rowton in Shropshire, which is eleven miles north-east of Shrewsbury and was then a chapelry in the parish of High Ercall.[5] The parish register confirms his own statement that on the Sunday following his birth he was baptized at High Ercall. The church suffered severely in the Civil War, and the present structure is largely of the nineteenth century; but the earlier font is preserved in St Giles's Church, Shrewsbury.

Baxter's father, also Richard, he describes as 'a mean Freeholder (called a Gentleman for his Ancestors sake, but of a small Estate, though sufficient)', which at this time was 'entangled by Debts'.[6]

Rowton was the parental home of Baxter's mother, Beatrice Adeney, and it was with his grandparents that he spent the first ten years of his life. This circumstance, which he does not explain, together with the facts that he left home for eighteen months when he was sixteen, and that his mother died when he was only nineteen, makes it easier to understand why his references to her are

1. D.W.L. MS., 5:11.   2. *57*, p. 543.   3. *2*, p. 521.   4. *112*, p. 1.
5. On the initiative of the parish council a modest monument to his memory was unveiled on the village green in June 1951.
6. *97*, p. 1; *R.B.*, I, i, §1.

so few and bare. Also, her place was quickly filled by a stepmother, who was to prove 'a Special Blessing to our Family', and towards whom to the end of her long life—she lived till 1680 and the great age of ninety-six—Baxter felt an admiring reverence.

His schooling at Rowton was worse than scanty. In six years he had as many as four masters, the successive 'readers' at the chapel. All of them, he says, were ignorant; two of them preached once a month, the other two never; and two were immoral, the last of them drinking 'himself, wife and children to be stark beggars'.[1]

The coronation of Charles I on 2 February 1626 was a day at school which the young Richard remembered, not only because, very properly, 'we had leave to play', but because (though in London, according to William Laud, it was 'a very bright sun-shining day') at Ercall 'at Two of the Clock . . . there happened an Earthquake'. Baxter was always interested in the natural phenomena which to him seemed supernatural. Shortly after this excitement he was removed to his parents' home about ten miles away at Eaton Constantine, 'a village most pleasantly and health-fully situate' in the parish of Leighton-under-Wrekin, close to 'Severn River, and five miles [actually eight]' south-east of Shrewsbury. Later in the century the black-and-white, half-timbered house became the home of Samuel Shute, a Nonconformist noted for being Sheriff of London in 1681, and in 1682 in prison; but it is remembered today as 'Baxter's House', and fifty years ago contained a settle bearing his parents' initials.[2]

So far as schooling went, the removal to Eaton at first brought no improvement. The 'reader', who was over eighty and 'never preached in his life', put in for one year a day-labourer, and for a second a tailor, to read for him. A succession of curates included the reader's son, 'a famous stage-player', and his grandson, who 'was unlearned and never preached'; then a lawyer's clerk, who was 'a common drunkard'; and a fourth, 'who being detected to be vicious, and have forged orders, fled'. These were the men who

---

1. *103*, pt i, p. 38f., naming the last three, but not the first, 'because he was allied to me'; cf. *R.B.*, I, i, §1. The school at Ercall was not founded till 1663.

2. In 1961, when the property changed hands, the house was described in the *Daily Telegraph* for 31 May as 'the principal residence on an arable and stock farm of 96 acres'. A photograph of the house faces p. xv of J. M. Lloyd Thomas's abridgement (1925) of *R.B.*

'taught school and tipled on the week-days, and whipt the boys when they were drunk'.[1] Strange teachers for one of the most learned and most earnest of seventeenth-century divines!

At Donnington, however, in the neighbouring parish of Wroxeter, 'that ancient Uriconium' with its 'Ruins and old Coin', there was a real school, under the patronage of the Newport family, who, though their chief house (rebuilt in 1608) was at High Ercall, lived in Wroxeter parish at Eyton-on-Severn. To this school Baxter went. Later there joined him in 'the highest form', of which he had long been 'chief', the son of a steward of Newport's, Richard Allestree, who in the years when Baxter was a Nonconformist became Regius Professor of Divinity at Oxford and eventually Provost of Eton. 'In a lower form' were the young Newports, Francis (later Earl of Bradford) and Andrew, memorials to whom may still be seen in Wroxeter Parish church.

Baxter himself was 'strongly possest . . . to have setled at the University';[2] but his schoolmaster, John Owen, had a friend at Ludlow, then the seat of the President of the Council of the Welsh Marches and Shrewsbury's rival as the capital of the West. This was Richard Wickstead, then Chaplain to the Council; and Owen persuaded his bright pupil, who ruefully confesses that he knew no better, that to become Wickstead's pupil would be 'better than the University'. At the age of sixteen, therefore, the boy left home and school for Ludlow. He was to be bitterly disappointed. Wickstead proved 'but a superficial scholar' and 'never read to me'; 'only he loved me'. One can hardly miss the pathos with which this last phrase is slipped in, especially if one reads further the account of the 'one intimate companion' of Baxter's youth, another lad in Ludlow. 'We walk'd together, we read together, we prayed together, and when we could we lay together. . . . He was the first that ever I heard pray *extempore* (out of the pulpit) and that taught me so to pray.' But alas!

> ther wil be blastings and blightings of hope
> and love, and rude shocks that affray.

Before they had been long acquainted, his friend had more than once fallen into 'a degree of drunkenness' that terrified Baxter; and eventually he became 'a fudler, and railer at strict men'. This

1. *103*, pt i, p. 39, naming them; cf. *R.B.*, I, i, §1; *71*, 1st pag., p. 901.
2. *134*, p. 9.

friend's fall evidently typified for Baxter what he felt to be the evil atmosphere of Ludlow and its council. He found the town 'full of temptations through the multitude of persons (counsellors, attorneys, officers and clerks), and much given to tipling and excess'. At the end of his life he recalled how he was 'strongly tempted to the love of cards and dice' himself, and for a time was overcome by the former. When he found he had 'no skill at tables', he asked the Clerk of the Kitchen, 'the best gamester in the house', to teach him 'for a price'. The result was doubly surprising. In their first contest Baxter won hands down. 'I perceived that it was the devil's temptation to draw me to be a gamester . . . and never plaid more.'[1] For once the devil had over-reached himself!

Baxter returned home, wiser, but in sadness not in learning. His parents, however, were no wiser; and Wickstead still wished to set him in 'a rising way'. His old schoolmaster was ill, and for three months Sir Richard Newport commissioned Baxter to take his place. One may surmise that Sir Richard had something to do with the next phase of Baxter's education; for Sir Henry Herbert, to whom Baxter now went in London, was his first cousin. Later in their lives Sir Richard and Baxter became distantly connected through Sir Robert Harley, for, while Harley's third wife, the famous Brilliana, was a first cousin of Baxter's stepmother, his second was Newport's sister; but there is no evidence that they renewed acquaintance.

London was to prove no more tolerable than Ludlow; but Baxter did not forget his debt to Sir Henry Herbert. In 1672, when he published a book animadverting on the *De Veritate* of Herbert's brother, Lord Herbert of Cherbury, he dedicated it to Sir Henry, acknowledging not only his 'personal ancient obligations' but the gift of the *De Veritate*.[2] He also allowed himself to express his regret that 'our supernatural Revelations and Verities' had not possessed Lord Herbert's soul with 'so sweet a gust, and fervent ascendent holy LOVE, as breatheth' in the poems of 'his and your holy and excellent Brother', George. Baxter's admiration for George Herbert was lifelong. One wonders if he knew that Lord Herbert had been born at Eyton-on-Severn, and had spent the first nine years of his life there with his grandparents, as Baxter

---

1. *135*, p. 251f.
2. Sir Henry also gave a copy to John Evelyn: *Dictionary of National Biography*, *s.v.* Herbert.

had done at Ercall; also if he ever admired the 'one Autumnall face' of the Herberts' mother on her effigy in Montgomery Church.

Sir Henry Herbert, in Whitehall, was at this time Master of the Revels. One of his duties was the licensing of plays for the theatre. 'He was very careful to excise all blasphemous language.'[1] Even so, the plays were more than the young man could stomach. When forty years later he came to write *The Christian Directory*, Baxter was careful to state that, however many and good the reasons for avoiding stage plays might be, attendance at the theatre was not, in itself, a sin; but—'a stage-play instead of a sermon on the Lord's-days in the afternoon'! London was corrupt. When after only a month Baxter's mother fell ill and desired his return, Baxter, nothing loth, went home; though in the event it meant that from Christmas 1634 till the following Easter he was to be 'shut up' in the house by 'the greatest Snow . . . that hath been in this Age', unable to escape from his mother's 'heart-piercing groans'. On 10 May she died, aged only forty.

The impression so far is of an eager, sensitive, intelligent boy; lovable, but perhaps rather lonely; certainly (by our standards) over-serious, more at home in the society of his elders than of his fellows. An only child, who had grown up at first with his grand-parents, he recalls no friends of his childhood other than the companion at Ludlow, whose lamentable defection must have driven him further into himself, to take more solitary walks up the Wrekin. He was certainly, from the beginning, a great reader: 'Delight in feigned Histories called Romances' he confesses, look-ing back, to have been 'my great, because my most delightful Sin'. Because of his equal delight in 'Apples, and Pears, and Plumbs and Cheese', he also admits, more than once, that 'sometime with a grudging Conscience, I ventured over the Hedge to a Neighbours Fruit'. This failing, 'a Sin that Austin himself confesseth',[2] he believed to have been punished by the gastric acidity which ruined his health as a grown man. He tells us 'my own nature was as much addicted to playfullness as most'.[3] He took his part in 'boxing with School-boys' and could recall 'one Man, whose Leg I hurt with playful Wrestling, when I was a Boy, which almost broke my heart

1. *Ibid.*
2. *134*, p. 8f.; cf. *R.B.*, I, i, §§1 (3) and 9.
3. *71*, 1st pag., p. 464.

with grief, though he was quickly cured';[1] but his references to 'children, busie in hunting butterflies'[2] or to 'a Footbal in the midst of a crowd of Boyes'[3] suggest (like Bridges's 'fortune of the football') the detached observer rather than the player. There is perhaps less detachment in his memories of the morris-dancers: 'I cannot forget . . . how hardly when I was young, I passed by the Dancing and the Playing Congregations.' The fact that one of his 'Fathers own Tenants was the Town Piper' must have made it the harder to hold aloof; and when he tells how 'sometimes the Morrice-Dancers would come into the Church, in all their Linnen and Scarfs and Antick Dresses, with Morrice-bells jingling at their leggs',[4] the dancing seems to move still in his writing, like the bell-ringing echoing in Bunyan's.

Looking back as a mature Christian to the first awakening of his soul and to the consequent doubts, temptations and perplexities through which he passed before 'God was pleased to give me some Peace and Comfort', Baxter knew well that God's ways are past finding out; and from one point of view 'God's Dealings are much what the same with all his Servants in the main'. Yet from another he remembered how uneasy he had been 'because I could not distinctly trace the Workings of the Spirit upon my heart' in the method approved by the best writers of his youth, 'nor knew the Time of my Conversion': 'whether sincere Conversion began now, or before, or after, I was never able to this day to know'. He had come to see that 'Education is God's ordinary way for the Conveyance of his Grace' and that 'the Soul of a Believer groweth up by degrees'. In any case, his interest in phenomenology, whether natural or supernatural, was so consuming that he could hardly refrain from setting down, more than once, 'just in what order I have received the christian religion' and the steps by which God was 'pleased to resolve me for himself'. 'God breaketh not all Mens hearts alike'; and Baxter was not loth 'to insert the transcript of my own experiences'.[5]

In the first place, he acknowledges as readily as any Quaker that 'I found a Power even in my Childhood, to awe my Soul, and check my sin and folly'. 'I took my Religion at first upon my

1. *106*, i, p. 3, cf. ii, p. 143: *R.B.*, I, ii, §258.
2. *57*, p. 244.
3. *2*, p. 818; cf. *57*, p. 244; *114*, p. 103.
4. *62*, p. 116f.
5. *57*, p. 204f.; cf. *R.B.*, I, i, §§213, 6 (3).

Parents word.' Even before his removal to his parents' home at
Eaton Constantine, 'when I was very young', his father's 'serious
speeches of God and the Life to come, possessed me with a fear of
sinning'; 'from the first of my remembrance I liked Religious
Goodness, and feared sinning since my Father had talkt to me of
God and Sin and the World to come'; 'God made him the
Instrument of my first Convictions, and Approbation of a Holy
Life, as well as of my Restraint from the grosser sort of Lives.'
Baxter's father had himself been converted 'by the bare reading of
the Scriptures in private, without either Preaching, or Godly
Company, or any other Books but the Bible'. To him the boy owed
it, above all, that he early came 'to love the Bible'. It was also
through his father that there came into his hands the devotional
books by which 'it pleased God to awaken my soul': an old torn
copy of Edmund Bunny's abridgement of the Jesuit Robert
Persons's *Book of Resolution,* which 'a poor Day-Labourer . . .
lent my Father'; Richard Sibbes's *Bruised Reed,* which his father
bought from 'a poor Pedlar' at the door; and a collection of some
works by William Perkins, which a servant in the house had.[1]
Later, Baxter's father joined him at Kidderminster,[2] and he is
sometimes included in greetings from Baxter's correspondents:
one of these asks for 'the (as it is called) first refusal'[3] of the house
at Eaton Constantine, should the present tenant leave it. It was
probably there that in the summer of 1661 Baxter visited him from
London, while on what proved to be his last visit to Kidderminster.
This was the last time that he saw his father, who was then 'aged'
and 'lying in great pain of the Stone and Strangury', for on
13 February 1663 he was buried at Leighton-under-Wrekin.[4]
Baxter's father is a shadowy figure. 'He was reviled commonly by
the Name of Puritan, Precisian and Hypocrite': from him, perhaps, came some of the sharpness and severity characteristic of
Baxter (as he often disarmingly admits and regrets), that tendency
to 'too much neglect of Ceremony, or humble Complement' which,
later, his wife 'would modestly tell me of'.[5] The severity of both
father and son is present, yet dissolved, in a charming passage
towards the end of William Bates's *Funeral-Sermon* for Baxter:

1. *Locc. cit.*; *134*, p. 8.
2. *R.B.*, I, i, §137 (28).
3. D.W.L. MS., 6:120.
4. *R.B.*, I, ii, §248; Powicke, i, appendix 1.
5. *97*, p. 70.

2

His Father said with Tears of Joy to a Friend, My Son Richard
I hope was sanctified from the Womb: for when he was a little Boy in
Coats, if he heard other Children in play speak profane Words, he would
reprove them to the Wonder of those that heard him.

Baxter's stepmother was Mary Huncks, sister of Sir Fulk
Huncks, Governor of Shrewsbury, and of Sir Henry Huncks,
Governor of Banbury, and first cousin of Edward, first Earl of
Conway, and of his sister Brilliana, Lady Harley, with whom she
lived at one time. Baxter describes his stepmother as 'a person of
. . . long and extraordinary holiness', 'having lived from her youth
in the greatest Mortification, Austerity to her Body, and constancy
of Prayer and all Devotion, of any one that ever I knew'.[1] Her
influence on him, though undoubtedly great during the years when
she also made one of his 'Family' at Kidderminster, did not begin
before his father's marriage to her in 1636, but may be held to
throw some light, obliquely, on his father's character. She long
outlived his father, for it was not until 31 August 1680 that she too,
now aged ninety-six, was buried at Leighton.[2] During her widow-
hood she lived at first in the old home at Eaton Constantine, but
latterly with Baxter, who 'wholly maintained' her. He allowed her,
he wrote early in 1680, 'now £20 per annum, and heretofore £16
these 17 years' from his 'small patrimony', which extended 'but to
five tenements of freehold'.[3]

Next after his father, Baxter names 'some Reverend peaceable
Divines' by whose acquaintance 'God was pleased much to comfort
and settle me'. As we have already had occasion to notice, the
condition of the ministry in general in the parishes near his home
was deplorable: 'within a few miles about us, were near a dozen
. . . Ministers that were near Eighty years old apiece, and never
preached; poor ignorant Readers, and most of them of Scandalous
Lives';[4] and it later became one of Baxter's primary aims, and
achievements, to assist in the effective remedying of such a state of
affairs. But 'three or four constant competent Preachers lived near
us . . . Conformable all save one', namely Humphrey Barnet, Curate
of Uppington; them the young man sought out and later gratefully

---

1. 97, epistle to reader; *R.B.*, III, ii, §67.
2. Powicke, i, appendix 1.
3. *R.B.*, III, i, §171; D. W. L. MS., 10:379 (cf. 6:178, 188 and 380);
141, 55: 'the bigger Tenement I let at £30 per annum'.
4. *R.B.*, I, i, §1; the paragraph in which (*103*, pt i, p. 38f.) Baxter later
filled out these charges in detail is a most lacerating passage.

acknowledged what he owed them. Only one of these was a man of any note, Samuel Smith, Curate of Cressage in the parish of Cound, whose expository and devotional writings, some of which Baxter names, were exceedingly popular, a meditation on a text in the Song of Songs reaching a thirty-second posthumous edition in 1682. 'This good Man,' Baxter writes, 'was one of my most familiar Friends, in whose Converse I took very much delight.' He evidently also formed an enduring friendship with Francis Garbett, 'the faithful, learned Minister at Wroxeter', for in 1651 Garbett wrote to him thanking him for the gift of each of his first three books, adding 'I know not why you should acknowledge your self so much beholden to me as in your letter you have done'.[1] The third of these ministers, a namesake of Baxter's, though seemingly no relation, was George Baxter, Rector of Little Wenlock, 'who lived there till about eighty six years of Age, in the constant faithful Preaching and practising of the Gospel'.[2] In 1647 all three men were approved for the presbyteries to be set up in Shropshire, and in 1648 all three signed the Shropshire Presbyterian ministers' manifesto entitled *A Testimony*. At the Restoration Samuel Smith lost, or left, his curacy at the age of seventy-six; and two of George Baxter's sons (as also two of Humphrey Barnet's) were among the clergy ejected in Shropshire or Worcestershire. From these few facts and characterisations it is not difficult to picture the piety which thus attracted and helped to form the young Baxter: it was marked by a concern for preaching and for discipline, and by a freedom from individualistic sectarianism combined with willingness to suffer for conscience' sake. Since George Baxter is the only one of the three men not described as 'learned', he (unless the reference is to Barnet) is probably the subject of the following reminiscence:

I remember my self that when I was young, I had sometime the company of one antient godly Minister, who was of weaker parts than many others, but yet did profit me more than most; because he would never in prayer or conference, speak of God or the life to come, but with such marvellous seriousness and reverence as if he had seen the Majesty and Glory which he talkt of.[3]

Here is the source and spring of a confession and exhortation to be found in Baxter's *Reformed Pastor*:

1. D.W.L. MSS., 6:120, 3:165. 2. *R.B.*, III, i, §202 (6).
3. *71*, 2nd pag., p. 101.

I know not what it doth by others; but the most Reverent Preacher, that speaks as if he saw the face of God, doth more affect my heart, though with common words, than an unreverent man with the most exquisite preparations. . . . We should as it were suppose we saw the Throne of God, and the millions of Glorious Angels attending him, that we might be awed with his Majesty.[1]

Garbett and Smith lent the boy books on discipline, in support of conformity, and from the one close companion at Ludlow he had learned to be 'unwearied in reading all serious Practical Books of Divinity'. At Ludlow he also had the run of Wickstead's library:

I had read a multitude of our English Practical Treatises, before I had ever read any other Bodies of Divinity.

Next Practical Divinity, no Books so suited with my Disposition as Aquinas, Scotus, Durandus, Ockam, and their Disciples; because I thought they narrowly searched after Truth, and brought Things out of the darkness of Confusion: For I could never from my first Studies endure Confusion!

I too much neglected the Study of Words.

Besides the Latin Tongue, and but a mediocrity in Greek (with an inconsiderable trial at the Hebrew long after) I had no great skill in Languages . . . And for the Mathematicks, I was an utter stranger to them.

Here too we see the father of the man. In an interesting comparative survey of the different disciplines and his acquaintance with them, composed in 1672, Baxter writes that 'all truth is useful: Mathematicks, which I have least of, I find a pretty manlike sport', and that 'I much value the method and sobriety of Aquinas, the subtility of Scotus and Ockam, the plainness of Durandus' but 'I feel my self much better in Herberts *Temple*: or in a heavenly treatise of faith and Love';[2] and in *A Christian Directory*, when recommending books for 'the Poorest or Smallest Library that is tolerable', he urges the acquisition of 'as many Affectionate Practical English Writers as you can get'.[3]

Baxter thus expected, or desired, that others' studies should be as his own, in which divinity 'always had the first and chiefest place'. At the same time, he was well aware that in his own case what in fact 'caused me to study Practical Divinity first, in the most Practical Books, in a Practical Order' was, to a considerable degree, the ill health which dogged him from boyhood and which,

1. *17*, p. 128.
2. *124*, p. 9.
3. *71*, 1st pag., p. 922.

by keeping him in constant expectation of death, forced him early
'to determine first of my Ultimate End'. Smallpox when fourteen
years of age and later a chronic cold and cough, nose-bleeding and
spitting of blood 'of two years continuance' had their effect on a
youth already naturally serious. 'The Face of Death, and nearness
of Eternity, did much convince me, what Books to read, what
Studies to prefer and prosecute, what Company and Conversation
to choose!' All this, so far from resenting, Baxter regarded (at least
in later life) as evidence of God's undeserved mercy,

causing me rather to groan under my infirmities, than to fight with
strong and potent Lusts. . . . Great Mercy hath trained me up all my
daies, since I was Nineteen years of Age [that is to say, from the winter
which ended with his mother's death], in the School of Affliction, to keep
my sluggish Soul awake in the constant expectations of my change.[1]
From the Age of 21 till near 23, my Weakness was so great, that I
expected not to live above a year.[2]

During these last two years, Baxter was further influenced,
indeed his future (humanly speaking) was determined, by the
devotion of a small group of Nonconformists then meeting in
Shrewsbury. Up to this time his piety, however intense in an
interior sense, had been outwardly conventional. He 'was satisfied
in the Matter of Conformity' and 'joyned with the Common-
Prayer with . . . hearty fervency'. When he was fifteen years old,
with 'thirty or fourty' other boys, he had been confirmed, or
'Bishopt as it was then called', by the Bishop of Lichfield, Thomas
Morton, for whom he always retained a regard as 'one of the
learned'st and best Bishops that ever I knew', a man of understanding and moderation.

We ran thither from School, without the Minister's knowledge, or
one word from our Master, to tell us what Confirmation is; and in a
Church-yard in the Path-way, as the Bishop past by, we kneeled down,
and laying his Hands on every Boys Head, he said a few words, I know
not what; nor did any one of my School-fellows, as far as I could
perceive, know what he said.

In these early years, he later confessed 'with shame', he also acted
as godfather, 'to one when I was a Child. . . . And to three more
when I was twenty three years of age.'[3] When Baxter met the
Shrewsbury Nonconformists, he was easily persuaded by his

1. *114*, p. 222: cf. *R.B.*, I, i, §§5 and 9.
2. *R.B.*, I, i, §16.
3. *29*, p. 155 (cf. *127*, p. 101); *127*, p. 68 (cf. *101*, p. 168).

minister friends, and by the books which he had from them, that 'the reasoning of the Nonconformists' was 'weak' and that 'the Conformists had the better Cause'. Even after he was ordained, though he soon became uneasy over three points of conformity, 'most of this I kept to myself', and at first 'daily disputed against the Nonconformists'.

Yet it is plain that the 'very zealous godly Nonconformists in Shrewsbury' made a deep impression on him by their 'fervent Prayers and savoury Conference and holy Lives'; and, in view of Baxter's eventual, though reluctant, acceptance of the necessity for Nonconformity, they deserve more than passing attention. The fact that the theology of the leading spirit among them, Walter Cradock, came increasingly under Baxter's disapproval ('how great an Antinomian he turned',[1] he wrote in 1684) made it difficult for him to acknowledge the effect at a formative moment in his life which Cradock and his friends had had; yet even then honesty, if not gratitude, compelled him to describe Cradock as 'a most zealous man for practical godliness', and in a tract published in the last year of his life his thoughts returned to the 'many excellent Christians in Shrewsbury', whom 'the Bishops severity against Private Meeting caused . . . to meet secretly for mutual Edification', 'when I was 21'.[2] At this time Cradock was in flight from the pursuivants of the Bishop of St Asaph, who was no more willing for him to be Curate at Wrexham than the Bishop of Llandaff had been for him to be Curate at Cardiff, where for refusing to read the *Book of Sports* enjoining the playing of games on the Lord's Day he had been suspended in 1634; and 'in Mr Rich. Simond's School in Shrewsbury, he was concealed from the Bishops pursuit, by the Name of Mr Williams'.[3] The schoolmaster, Richard Symonds, was himself 'a suspended priest driven out of North Wales'; later he became, with Cradock, a leader in the movement to evangelise Wales, a cause which, as we shall see, Baxter also had much at heart. Two others in the group are named by Baxter: George Fawler, who in 1643 became chaplain of the Bridewell Hospital in London, where he continued till 1662, when he was ejected under the Act of Uniformity; and Michael Old, who according to Baxter was 'for

1. *118*, 'Account', p. 28.
2. *132*, p. 539.
3. *118*, 'Account', p. 28; *Dictionary of National Biography*, *s.v.* Symonds, and other writers have wrongly taken the phrase 'in Mr Rich. Simond's School' to apply to Baxter.

zeal known through much of England'. After the Restoration both these men continued faithful to their nonconforming principles; for in 1672, when under the royal indulgence of that year Fawler had his house at Islington licensed for Nonconformist worship, Old's house at Sheriffhales was licensed likewise.

The natural attraction which this earnest company exerted upon the young Baxter seemed approved as by their drawing together through a divine purpose when he discovered that for Fawler and Old, as well as for himself, 'the first lively motions that awakened their Souls to a serious resolved care of their Salvation, was the reading of Bunny's *Book of Resolution*'.[1] What evidently affected him most was their praying.

> Before the Parliament began, how frequent and fervent were we in secret: . . . O the earnest prayers that I have heard in secret daies heretofore for a Painful Ministry, and for Discipline! As if they had even wrestled for salvation itself? Yea they commonly called Discipline, the Kingdom of Christ; or the Exercise of his Kingly office in his Church; and so preached and prayed for it, as if the setting up of Discipline, had been the setting up of the Kingdom of Christ.[2]

The friends did not long continue together in Shrewsbury. Before December 1638, when Baxter was ordained deacon, Fawler had accepted a Shropshire curacy at Uffington; and by February 1639 Cradock and Symonds had removed to neighbouring counties where, under Sir Robert Harley's protection, Symonds became schoolmaster at Brampton Bryan, while Cradock was presented to the living of Llanfairwaterdine. Cradock was soon cited afresh and forced to flee; but by assisting later that year at Llanvaches in Monmouthshire in the formation of the first Independent church in Wales he at last realised something of what he and his friends in Shrewsbury had been planning and praying for. The gathering of a separatist congregation was not Baxter's conception of the setting up of the Kingdom of Christ, now or at any time in his life. Yet he shared with these men, he perhaps even first caught from them, the passionate concern for a discipline through which Christ's rule in his Church might be a reality. He also came to realise, with discomfort, that in their eyes bishops were, primarily, persecutors, and to think that 'those that silenced and troubled

---

1. *132*, p. 540.
2. *17*, p. 378f.; cf. the memory in 'my younger years' of 'some godly persons in and neer Shrewsbury' recorded by William Voile, *A Glasse and Salve for Professors* (1668), p. 44 (with reference to Cradock, p. 31).

such Men could not be the genuine Followers of the Lord of Love'. Above all, he never forgot their prayers. He was aware of 'Disorder and Repetitions and unfit Expressions' in 'the Prayers of many a weak Christian that I have heard'; but he was equally aware of 'Disorder and Defectiveness' in the Prayer Book.[1] Some years later he would write with feeling of some 'laymen that were humble praying persons only' that 'God did not deny their prayers, though they were without Book, and such as some deride as extemporate'.[2]

There is one further vital influence to be recorded, that of the man because of whom Baxter entered the Christian ministry. It is intriguing that this was neither one of the learned ministers who had won his regard nor a friend who joined him in taking orders, but James Berry, a man who, with origins obscurer than Baxter's, rose to a position of great responsibility in the world of politics, becoming in 1655 the Protector's Major-General for Wales and the Border Counties and two years later a member of the House of Lords. In the former capacity he wins S. R. Gardiner's commendation for his compassion and kindliness of heart, particularly in his treatment of the religious enthusiasts of his area, whom he defended as 'an affectionate, tender-spirited people that want judgment' and more than once released when, after arrest, they were brought before him. Even the Quakers allowed on one occasion that 'Hee discoursed vs Loveingly, and was Curteous to vs in his Carriage', while another wrote that the Major-General 'hath spoken much in the behalf of Friends, which keeps down the persecuting spirits in these parts'.[3]

Baxter's account of his relations with Berry takes some unravelling and is perhaps not quite ingenuous. In September 1659 he dedicated his *Treatise of Self-Denyall* to Berry not only as his 'ancient, dearest friend' to whom he had 'the same affections as heretofore', but as his 'late monitor', who 'provoked me to this sweet, though flesh-displeasing life of the ministry'. 'You brought me into the ministry': 'I doubt not but many thousand souls will thank you, when they have here read that you were the man that led me into the ministry.' Yet when in the first part of his auto-

1. *R.B.*, I, i, §17, ii, §174 and i, §19.
2. 97, p. 9: cf. *R.B.*, I, i, §133.
3. MS. printed in *First Publishers of Truth*, edited by N. Penney (1907), p. 282, confirming Gardiner's conjecture in *History of Commonwealth and Protectorate*, iv, p. 10; Swarthmore MSS., I: 201.

biography, composed in 1664–5, he came to write of his entering the ministry, Baxter says nothing of this; only that 'James Berry (who lived in the House with me, and had lived with him)' was the means of his appointment by Richard Foley to be schoolmaster at Dudley—this being the title upon which he was ordained—and that 'Mr Foley and James Berry' accompanied him to Worcester for his ordination. In a later paragraph about Berry, which incidentally provides the information that Berry was also involved in the invitation to him later to become chaplain to 'Cromwell's old Troop', Baxter has the honesty to call Berry 'my old bosom Friend, that had lived in my House, and been dearest to me', but he then proceeds to a lengthy condemnation of Berry as 'taking his Light among the Sectaries' and thus 'forsaking his own Opinions' (by contrast with himself, 'who adhereth to the way which *he* forsaketh') and even, in fine, as 'one that taketh Errour for Truth, and Evil to be Good'.[1]

Although in the dedicatory epistle to his book of 1659 Baxter already shows uneasiness over Berry's character, the change of tone after only five years is so marked that one can hardly escape the suspicion that he no longer desired to acknowledge all that he owed to a man who at the Restoration was, in Baxter's own phrase, 'one of the first that fell' and who, after a period of imprisonment, was now in obscurity. The phrase in Baxter's analysis of Berry's character, 'when Cromwell made him his Favourite', and the position of the paragraph, following as it does an equally acid (and better known) paragraph in analysis of Cromwell, are also revealing. He had been bitterly disappointed in both men and could not forgive either for some share (as he saw it) in spoiling the other. Of Cromwell he believed that 'Prosperity and Success corrupted him': 'it is commonly seen', he quoted from Bacon's *Essays*, 'that Men once placed take in with the contrary Faction to that by which they enter'. Probably Baxter's refusal of the invitation to Cromwell's regiment had led to estrangement from Berry as well as from Cromwell.

Although in 1657, when Berry was in power, Baxter could still go to him for support in his scheme for a university for Wales, and Berry then 'promised me his best assistance',[2] two years earlier,

---

1. *R.B.*, I, i, §83.
2. D.W.L. MS., 1:127; printed in Merioneth Historical and Record Society *Journal*, II, ii (November 1954).

when Berry had ordered a number of arrested Quakers to be released, Baxter, who had recently been interrupted by Quakers while preaching and who was present at the interview, did not approve: Baxter 'only stood by the fire side with his Hatt over his eyes', a Quaker witness records, '& said nothing'.[1] Yet the charge that Berry's support of the sectaries implied a change in his convictions may not be true. He did not change later, for of the church ministered to by the Congregational divine, John Owen, with which he was worshipping when in 1659 it met at Wallingford House, he continued a member after the Restoration when, now Nonconformist, it met in Leadenhall Street; and it is possible that in 1636-7 he was one of the Nonconformists in Shrewsbury and that it was here that Baxter met him. Some support for this conjecture lies in the following considerations: first, that ten years later Berry knew and respected Walter Cradock;[2] secondly, that, since his position was that of 'a Clark of Iron-works',[3] he presumably lived in a town; and thirdly, that a letter from him to Baxter immediately after Baxter's ordination, praying that God might 'enable you to that great work whereunto he hath called you', which opens 'Charissime amice' and is subscribed 'yours if his own',[4] was written from Shrewsbury.

However we may interpret their original close friendship or their subsequent estrangement, Berry not only persuaded Baxter to take orders but found him his post as 'first School-master', 'with an Usher' to assist him, in the school newly founded by Richard Foley at Dudley, Worcestershire. Foley was an ironmaster at Stourbridge, then the centre of the iron industry in the Midlands, where he founded a highly successful business. Baxter's statements, in one place that Major-General Berry 'had formerly lived as a Servant (a Clark of Iron-Works)' and in another that he 'had lived with' Foley, make it plausible that in 1638 Berry was, or till recently had been, in Foley's employ. Baxter's introduction to Foley as his 'first Patron' was of greater importance than the brevity of his stay at Dudley, where he lived with Foley's son

1. *First Publishers of Truth*, p. 285.
2. *State Papers of John Thurloe*, ed. T. Birch (1742), iv, p. 565.
3. *R.B.*, I, i, §143.
4. D.W.L. MS., 4:194; printed in Sir J. Berry and S. G. Lee, *A Cromwellian Major General*, Oxford, 1938, pp. 7ff.: the earliest letter in the collection of Baxter's correspondence at Dr Williams's Library London, and the only letter from Berry preserved.

Richard, and his wife, might suggest; for Foley was also the founder of a considerable family (which in 1776 obtained 'one of the earliest industrial peerages'),[1] and when in 1657 he died, leaving a monument still to be seen in the church at Old Swinford (the parish of Stourbridge), his patronage of Baxter was continued by his son Thomas, whose friendship was as faithful after the Restoration as before. Thomas Foley was High Sheriff of Worcestershire in 1658 and M.P. for Bewdley in 1660: two of his daughters married two of Sir Robert Harley's sons, and a third married first a Knightley of Fawsley and secondly a Hampden. The possession of a patron in such positions and with such connections was not without its importance for Baxter. Baxter in turn had a sincere regard not only for Thomas Foley, who before his death in 1677 (his monument is in the parish church at Great Witley) followed his father's example in founding a school for poor boys (the Old Swinford Hospital), but for Foley's surviving sons, 'all three Religious worthy men'[2] and eventually all Members of Parliament.

On 23 December 1638 Baxter was ordained deacon at Worcester by the Bishop of Worcester, John Thornborough. The ordination certificate, together with the licence to teach at Dudley, granted five days earlier by the bishop's vicar-general, James Littleton, is still extant.[3] Thornborough was then seventy-seven years old and unable to use his hands. In the course of a correspondence during 1653 with 'one of the most learned of the Prelatists',[4] Martin Johnson, on the nature and necessity of ordination, Baxter throws in the following thinly veiled reminiscence of his own ordination:

The Bishop that was last save one in this Diocess was so lame of the Gout, that he could not move his Hand to ones Head, and though his Chaplain did his best to help him, yet I could not well tell whether I might call it Imposition of Hands when I saw it: Yet I never heard any

1. *Manchester Guardian*, 3 July 1951. The family's present representative is the eighth Lord Foley of this creation (an earlier creation of 1712 had become extinct in 1766).
2. *R.B.*, III, i, §202 (22); cf. *141*, p. 42f.
3. See *Baxter Treatises*, edited by R. Thomas, 1959, p. 5a.
4. *R.B.*, III, i, §202 (14), as living at Wombourn, Staffs, with the vicar, Thomas Willesby, at whose settlement there in October 1652 Baxter had been present (D.W.L. MS., 4:90); the identification with Martin Johnson is made virtually certain by the facts that most of Johnson's letters were written from, and one of Baxter's addressed to, Wombourn and that Johnson and Willesby were both natives of Spalding, Lincs, and both graduates of Emmanuel College, Cambridge.

on that Ground, suspect a nullity in his Ordination: Nor do I think that a Bishop loseth all his Power of Ordination if he lose his Hands, or the Motion of them.[1]

As against Johnson, who held 'the Necessity of Episcopal Ordination', Baxter held that ' it was not necessary *ad esse Ecclesiae*'. He here states that he was 'far from believing Imposition of Hands essential to Ordination'. In a later correspondence about ordination in general, he says 'I think ordination necessary *ordinis gratia, necessitate praecepti et medii* where it may be had; but not necessary *simpliciter* to the office'.[2]

He never mentions any further ordination, and no certificate of his ordination to the priesthood is extant. For reasons which are not clear, F. J. Powicke held that 'the known facts preclude the possibility of his having proceeded to the priesthood' and judged that 'it would appear that the defect in his Orders escaped' notice.[3] The present writer would argue the other way. All his life Baxter had a keen respect for law and a desire to 'do nothing disorderly, nor without Authority from Man, so far as belongs to them to convey it'.[4] At the Restoration he was not opposed to episcopal ordination in itself, nor did he then suggest his lack of it as a ground for his inability to conform. On the contrary, 'I have Episcopal Ordination,'[5] he wrote in 1682. Had he in fact lacked priest's orders, it seems unlikely that in 1660 the Earl of Clarendon would have offered him the see of Hereford, and almost certain that Charles II would not have accepted him as a chaplain, or the Bishop of London have licensed him to preach within the diocese. We may suppose that he was ordained priest either by Thornborough, or after Thornborough's death in 1641 by his successor, John Prideaux.

Baxter was only nine months at Dudley, and he does not say what success, or pleasure, he had in his work as schoolmaster in Foley's school there; but he there 'first preached occasionally'— his 'first Publick sermon' was delivered 'in the upper Parish Church', i.e. St Edmund's—and forty years later he still remembered Dudley with pleasure 'because of the great congregations of

1. *R.B.*, appendix ii, p. 35.
2. D.W.L. MS., 1:30.
3. *The Times Literary Supplement*, 22 January and 5 February 1925, pp. 56 and 88.
4. *R.B.*, appendix ii, p. 29.
5. *R.B.*, III, ii, §76 (misnumbered 79, p. 193).

a willing poor people that used there to crowd for instruction'. Here, where he discovered his power as a preacher, Baxter retained his hold over the 'poor tractable People'; for when later he went from Kidderminster to take part in a 'Monthly Lecture' established at Dudley, 'the poor Nailers and Labourers would not only crowd the Church as full as ever I saw any in London, but also hang upon the Windows, and the Leads without'.[1]

In the autumn of 1640 Baxter left Dudley for Bridgnorth, then 'the second Town of Shropshire' and a royal peculiar, 'priviledged from all Episcopal Jurisdiction, except the Archbishop's Triennial Visitation', 'to preach there as Assistant to the worthy Pastor', William Madstard, who was also the Ordinary, with jurisdiction over the six parishes within the peculiar. To his 'dearly beloved friends, the inhabitants of Bridgnorth', Baxter eleven years later dedicated the second part of *The Saints Everlasting Rest*, 'in testimony of his unfeigned love to them, who were the first to whom he was sent, as fixed, to publish the gospel'. Among these friends were three who later took orders: the schoolmaster, in whose house he lived, Richard Swaine, later Rector of Clyro, Radnorshire; Swaine's successor, Simon King, later Rector of Bottlebridge, Huntingdonshire; and one who was then a boy in the school, John Warren, later Vicar of Hatfield Broad Oak, Essex.[2]

Baxter's extant correspondence includes letters from Swaine and Warren but apparently none from any others whose friendship with him began at Bridgnorth. He acknowledges indeed that his labours there were 'not so successful as they proved afterwards in other places'. 'The People proved a very ignorant, dead-hearted People': 'their tipling and ill company and dead-heartedness quickly drowned all'. Other than the 'liberty of preaching the Gospel' afforded by 'the great Privileges of the place', he had no pleasure in remembering his 'year and three quarters' there. Bridgnorth 'made me resolve that I would never more go among a People that had been hardened in unprofitableness under a powerful Ministry'.[3] Madstard, who on other counts seems to have

---

1. *R.B.*, I, i, §§20, 136; D.W.L. MS., 4:232.
2. See *R.B.*, I, i, §26; III, i, §208 (15); I, i, §61; III, i, §208 (9); I, i, §156; and *41*, p. 293. Bottlebridge, *alias* Botolph's Bridge, is now united with Orton Longueville.
3. *R.B.*, I, i, §§21, 26, 29 and 30, corrected from MS.; D.W.L. MS., 4:232. The threefold repetition of 'dead-hearted' in a single paragraph is so unlike Baxter as effectively to suggest his misery at Bridgnorth.

been a man of pusillanimous spirit, was 'afflicted' with the 'dead-hearted unprofitable People' and spent most of his time in with-drawal outside the town. When, within a few weeks of Baxter's removal to Kidderminster, Madstard died of fever, but also, Baxter seems to imply, brokenhearted by his people's 'obdurate-ness', Baxter returned to Bridgnorth to preach the funeral sermon. Taking Ezekiel 33:33 for his text, he 'could not then suppress' his 'fears of some heavy Judgment to come upon that place'; and in 1646 the Parliament's forces 'burnt down the Town to the Ground, and burnt also the great Church where I preached that Sermon, and where Mr Madstard was interred'. Some years later Baxter came to Bridgnorth to preach again. He took the same text, 'to call their sins against their faithful Pastor to remembrance'; and this time the people as well as himself were 'much interrupted with Tears'. Today the inhabitants of the town take pleasure in pointing out 'Baxter's House' to the north-west of the churchyard. Did Baxter himself ever gaze at what is almost the only other house to have escaped the fire of 1646, the house 'Erected by R.For.1580' in the Cartway which was later to be the birthplace of Bishop Percy[1] of *The Reliques*? For the man who built it, Richard Forester, secretary to Bishop Bonner, was Baxter's great-grandfather.

During this period of preparation for his life's work Baxter, perhaps to his surprise, for he did not change his opinions easily, found that his sympathies were moving from a conventional Puritanism in the direction of Nonconformity. 'The promiscuous giving of the Lord's Supper' troubled him, and at Bridgnorth, where he was still only an 'Assistant', he 'never administred the Lord's Supper'. He also never 'Baptized any Child with the Sign of the Cross, nor ever wore the surplice'; and on this account, and also because he would not 'pray against the Scots (who were then upon their Entrance into England)', he was delated to the Earl of Bridgewater as Lord President of the Council of Wales and the Marches. Bridgewater replied correctly, however, 'that he had not the Ecclesiastical Jurisdiction', and therefore 'could not meddle', and Bridgnorth's privileged position saved Baxter from being 'put to appear at any Bishop's Court'. 'Kneeling at the Sacrament', he says, 'I thought lawful', and 'the Ring in Marriage I made no

---

1. The Librarian of Christ Church, Oxford, points out to me that the exhibition with which Percy went to Christ Church was founded by a kinsman of Baxter's wife.

Scruple about'. 'A Form of Prayer and Liturgy', also, 'I judged to be lawful, and in some Cases lawfully imposed'; but 'to Subscribe, *Ex Animo*, That there is nothing in the three Books contrary to the Word of God, was that, which if it had been to do again, I durst not do'. Most of all, he now came to 'deeper Thoughts of the Point of Episcopacy' and to judge 'the English Diocesan frame' as 'guilty of the Corruption of Churches and Ministry, and of the ruine of the true Church Discipline, and substituting a heterogeneal thing in its stead'. When in 1662 the Act of Uniformity demanded an unqualified acceptance of the Prayer Book and of diocesan episcopacy, Baxter's opposition to both, though in the interval left untried, was thus in principle of twenty years' standing.

This development in his thought was brought to a head by the oath against any alteration in the contemporary diocesan episcopal government of the Church demanded of clergy by convocation in 1640. Baxter opposed the oath at a meeting of ministers at Bridgnorth. But he had also been reading avidly. At Dudley he had come across more Nonconformists, 'godly honest People', who 'lent me Manuscripts and Books which I never saw before', one of these being perhaps a manuscript piece by Thomas Cartwright, which was later in Baxter's possession, though it is not among his MSS. at Dr Williams's Library. He 'laboured continually to repress' these Nonconformists' 'Censoriousness, and the boldness and bitterness of their Language against the Bishops'; but his antipathy to episcopacy as practised was strengthened, as earlier at Shrewsbury, by 'their sufferings from the Bishops'. As he wrote thirty years later, 'whoever be the Sect-Masters, it is notorious, That the Prelates (tho' not they only) are the Sect-Makers'.[1]

At Bridgnorth Baxter read further, both in Latin and in English, books on church government sent him by his 'very dear Friend', William Rowley, a draper and alderman of Shrewsbury. Rowley was a relative of William Madstard—it may have been he who suggested Baxter for Bridgnorth—and Baxter was with him when the news reached them of Madstard's death.[2] Rowley's Mansion, a fine brick house erected in 1618 and 'said to be the first house built

1. *R.B.*, I, i, §§19 and 22; III, i, §99; *100*, preface, fol. A2 verso; *71*, 1st pag., p. 853 margin. For a paper by Baxter justifying kneeling at the sacrament, dated 26 September 1639 and perhaps the earliest MS. in his autograph, see *Baxter Treatises*, ed. R. Thomas, p. 5a.
2. *R.B.*, I, i, §§22 and 30; Rowley's son Roger was also among Baxter's friends: *32* (9th ed.), p. 168, margin.

of that material' in the town, is 'perhaps the most interesting of all the old houses in Shrewsbury'.[1] Though now a museum, it has memories of Dr Johnson's friend, Dr Adams, who, as Vicar of St Chad's, lived in it from 1732 to 1775. One would like to think that, when Johnson visited Adams in 1774, he heard something of Rowley and Rowley's friendship with Baxter.

In April 1641 Baxter left Bridgnorth for Kidderminster, and it is with Kidderminster and with Worcestershire that his name has become inseparably intertwined. Yet he never forgot, or disowned, Shropshire. In a letter of 1658, written in passionate indignation to a mockingly recalcitrant parishioner, he discloses that the invitation to Kidderminster was not the only invitation which he received. 'I forsook the motion of the best place in Shrewsbury (my native county, a richer and more eminently religious people) to come hither'[2]—the reference is perhaps to St Alkmund's, from which Baxter's acquaintance, Thomas Good (later Master of Balliol College, Oxford), was ejected in 1645—and his 'desires of the prosperity of Christ's Church in Shrewsbury' remained constant, as his correspondence shows. 'I do assure you, impartially,' he wrote in 1652, 'that were I loose, I know not one congregation in England that I would sooner choose'[3] than St Mary's, Shrewsbury; and four years later, 'I confess I take Shrewsbury for as convenient a seat as almost any in England.'[4] When striving to bring about the founding of a university for Wales, he more than once let it be known that he considered 'the only fitt place in many respects' to be 'the healthful seat'[5] of Shrewsbury. To 'the inhabitants of the town of Shrewsbury . . . as also of the neighbouring parts' he dedicated the last part of The Saints Everlasting Rest, 'as a testimony of his love to his native soil, and to his many godly and faithful friends there living'. Among these were his distant cousin and 'special friend', the Governor of Coventry, John Barker,

1. Thomas Auden, Shrewsbury (2nd ed., 1923), p. 256; H. E. Forrest, The Old Houses of Shrewsbury, Shrewsbury (1935), p. 52, with illustration.
2. D.W.L. MS., 4:126.
3. See H. Owen and J. B. Blakeway, History of Shrewsbury (1825), ii, p. 379: the editors comment that Baxter 'charged himself, in some measure, with the care of all the churches of Shropshire'; for an appeal for help with Bridgnorth, cf. D.W.L. MS., 4:90.
4. Autobiography of Henry Newcome, edited by R. Parkinson, Chetham Society, o.s., 27 (1852), ii, p. 330.
5. D.W.L. MS., 1:127; cf. 27, preface to nobility and gentry, fol. f4 verso.

from Haughmond in the parish of Uffington, with whom he lived when in Coventry, and his 'most intire and dear friend', Colonel Sylvanus Taylor, from Harley, across the river from Eaton Constantine, with whom he would stay when in London. Richard Pigot, 'chief School-master' of the 'gallant free Schoole' in Shrewsbury, also became an 'old Friend'.[1] From Shropshire also Baxter would take his wife.

1. *3* (3rd ed.), preface, fol. ci and p. 210; *R.B.*, III, i, §208 (14).

CHAPTER 2

The Army Chaplain

IN THE middle of March 1641 Baxter received two letters inviting him to become 'preacher or lecturer' 'in the Parish Church of Kidderminster', and 'that satisfaction (so near as possible) may be given to all', 'to come over for your further approbation and trial . . . on Thursday next in the morning . . . to exercise amongst us'. The first of these letters bore eleven signatures: the second, written a day later, bore three more and explained the choice of Thursday as 'our Market day and also a day wherein we desire a weekly lecture'.[1]

This invitation was not from the patron of the living; nor was the living vacant. For some years now, despite royal and episcopal opposition, the middle-class laymen, in whose independent spirit and initiative much of the strength of Puritanism lay, had been supplementing, or defeating, the parochial organisation of the Church, with its normal system of patronage and episcopal over-sight, by taking upon themselves to invite, and to be financially responsible for, additional 'lecturers' or 'preachers', whose preach-ing (and sometimes whose life) they hoped to find more inspiring, or more satisfying, than that of their incumbents. Even so, the situation at Kidderminster had its anomalies.

In 1628, when George Dance had come to be vicar of the parish, the patron was Sir Edward Blount, a member of one of the many notable county families in Worcestershire which had remained Roman Catholic and were thereby disabled, by a law passed by way of retort to the Gunpowder Plot, from presenting to the benefice, Worcestershire being one of the counties in which the right to do so was then made over from papist patrons to the University of Oxford. Blount had died in 1630, and in Baxter's time at Kidderminster the patron was Colonel John Bridges, who, after he came to live in the town, became one of Baxter's staunchest supporters; but he was 'Governour of Warwick Castle . . . almost all the time of the Wars' and at this time still had his home at

1. D.W.L. MSS., 1:212 and 6:45.

Edstone Hall, near Alcester.[1] The man of influence in Kidder-minster, at least after Blount's death, was the Lord of the Manor and High Steward of the Borough, Sir Ralph Clare, of Caldwell Hall. Clare was a 'chief Friend' of the vicar. A number of the parishioners, however, were bitterly dissatisfied alike with the vicar and his curates, Dide and Turner. Turner, who was in charge of the chapelry at Mitton, two miles away, was 'a Drunkard, and a Railer, and the Scorn of the Country [i.e. county]', whose 'Trade on the Week-days was unlawful Marriages'. Of Dance himself the parishioners complained that he 'preached but once a quarter, which was so weakly, as exposed him to laughter' and also that 'he frequented Alehouses, and had sometimes been drunk'; while John Dide was even 'more offensive . . . than the Vicar to the Religious people'.[2]

Such conditions, and dissatisfaction with them, were in no way confined to Kidderminster. With the meeting of the Long Parliament in November 1640 and the setting up of a 'Committee for Scandalous Ministers', 'multitudes in all Countreys [i.e. counties] came up with Petitions against their Ministers'. To avoid the ignominy and possible consequences of exposure in the petition against his curates and himself drawn up by the parishioners, the Vicar of Kidderminster came to an unusual agreement with them: namely, that Dide should be replaced by another curate, to be a 'Preacher' whom he would 'not hinder from preaching . . . when-ever he pleased', to whom he would allow £60 per annum out of the £200 which his rich living provided, and who should be chosen by fourteen of the parishioners as feoffees or representative trustees in the business. In token of good faith, Dance even went so far as to sign a bond for £500, which is still extant.[3] This agreement was reached 'by the mediation of Sir Henry Herbert', now M.P. for Bewdley, where he lived at Ribbesford Hall. As Baxter's London friend in his youth Herbert may further have supported the inten-tion to invite him to Kidderminster; in 1657 he was lending Baxter books and discussing them with him.[4]

The letters which Baxter received, the signatories to which were the fourteen feoffees, were written a month after the date of

1. *135*, p. 37.
2. *R.B.*, I, i, §§129 and 29 and III, i, §150; *103*, p. 40; *134*, p. 57; cf. *101*, p. 72.
3. See *Baxter Treatises*, edited by R. Thomas, p. 5a.
4. See *R.B.*, appendix iii, p. 54.

Dance's bond. Although they did not say so, Baxter later discovered that he was their second choice. Their first had been a
much older man, Anthony Lapthorne, who was to become a leading Puritan in County Durham as Rector of the wealthy living of
Sedgefield; but Lapthorne's 'roughness and great immethodical-
ness, and digressions' had 'so offended the intelligent party' at
Kidderminster 'that they rejected him somewhat uncivilly, to his
great displeasure'. The 'approbation and trial' was thus not a
formality; but some of the feoffees knew Baxter already, and the
first letter was subscribed 'your affectionate friends'.

Instead of going over to Kidderminster on the Thursday, as they
suggested, Baxter replied with some conditions on his side, such as
'a house convenient';[1] and, being satisfied by a further letter bearing ten signatures—among them those of at least two parishioners
whose sons he was to see sent up to Cambridge and into the
ministry—besides those of five of the feoffees, he went to preach,
as was now requested, on Sunday, 4 April. The following day a
paper was drawn up, signed by Daniel Dobyns, High Sheriff of
the County in the following year, all fourteen feoffees and twelve
other parishioners, certifying that Baxter was 'chosen, elected and
nominated . . . preacher and Lecturer'.[2] This certificate is still
extant. It would seem that the parishioners also gave Baxter an
undertaking of a more personal nature, for in *The Saints Everlasting
Rest* he addresses them thus: 'do you not remember, that when you
called me to be your Teacher, you promised me under your hands,
that you would faithfully and conscionably endeavor the receiving
every truth, and obeying every command, which I should from the
Word of God manifest to you?'[3]

In the eyes of the law Baxter went to Kidderminster as curate to
George Dance, in succession to Dide, whom the vicar now 'put out'
—in 1660 he became Rector of Wigginton, Oxfordshire—and whom
an offensive parishioner could thus speak of as 'your predecessor'.[4]
His real status was in any case regularised in the following autumn
by an order of the House of Commons approving the establishment
of 'lecturers' and their maintenance at the parishioners' own
charge. It was, even so, an ambiguous and insecure position, and
one may wonder at the alacrity with which Baxter accepted it. It

1. D.W.L. MS., 3:111.
2. *Ibid.*, 3:112.
3. *2*, p. 601.
4. *134*, p. 71; D.W.L. MS., 4:124.

is true that he had no desire to stay in Bridgnorth. He says himself, 'I was naturally of a discouraged Spirit, so that if I had preached one Year, and seen no Fruits of it, I should hardly have forborn running away like Jonah, but should have thought that God called me not to that Place.'[1] But why did he choose Kidderminster out of 'so many great tenders'?[2]

Part of the answer, paradoxically but sensibly, is that he counted the deplorable state of affairs under George Dance as a ground for hope of success. The Bridgnorth congregation had been 'hardened in unprofitableness under a powerful Ministry';[3] the fact that at Kidderminster he 'came to a People that never had any awakening Ministry before (but a few formal cold Sermons of the Curate)'[4] Baxter put first among his many advantages there. Another part of the answer is surprising in one so much of whose fame, in his lifetime as well as posthumously, was to come from the ideals which he both held and put into practice as a 'Reformed Pastor'. The prospect that at Kidderminster he would officially have no pastoral responsibilities actually attracted Baxter. At the time of his ordination 'I can truly say', he writes, 'that a fervent desire of winning Souls to God was my motive'; but he admits that he 'had no inclination' to 'a Pastoral Charge'.[5]

His reading at Dudley and Bridgnorth led him, further, into difficulties over the administration of the sacraments. It was not only baptising with the sign of the cross which he 'thought Dr Ames proved unlawful'.

I never baptized but two Children [he wrote in 1650], and both those of godly Parents: Before I proceeded any further in the practice, I grew into doubts of the lawfullness of it.... This was about ten or eleven yeers ago; since which time I have . . . suspended my practice.

I bless God . . . that gave me still a detestation of Schism, and a high esteem of the Churches unity and peace; or else I had certainly turned Anabaptist.

[Nevertheless] I silently forbore the practice, . . . though I testified my approbation by my presence at the ordinance.

This is an astonishing confession from one who became noted as a leading writer in defence of infant baptism; and it says much for

---

1. *R.B.*, I, i, §136.　　　2. D.W.L. MS., 3:111.
3. *R.B.*, I, i, §29, corrected from MS.
4. *R.B.*, I, i, §137 (1): the curate's name, 'Mr Dide', is in MS., but erased.
5. *3* (3rd ed.), preface, fol. b3.

Baxter's ingenuous integrity that he printed such a confession at the beginning of his first work on the subject, *Plain Scripture Proof of Infants Church-membership and Baptism*. 'And being more in doubt about the other Sacrament than this,' he adds, 'I durst not adventure upon a full Pastoral charge, but to preach only as a Lecturer, till I were fully resolved.' Nor did he arrive at 'a full resolution' in favour of infant baptism until later, after reading 'all the Books for Rebaptizing that I could get'[1] while at Coventry.

In his first days at Kidderminster it was, indeed, not only the rightness of infant baptism which Baxter doubted. He still had to experience the agonising period through which many young ministers pass during their days at college. For a time he came 'to question the certain Truth of the Sacred Scriptures; and also the Life to come, and Immortality of the Soul', till he was drawn even towards 'a setled doubting of Christianity'. His continued reading contributed to this, but also his continued ill health; for 'since the day that I first preached [the] Gospel, I expected not . . . to live above a Year'.[2] Fortunately, from the 'beginning of my ministry at Kidderminster . . . I had a praying people, who were importunate with God on my behalf, in all my . . . weaknesses of body'; and 'when in very great weaknesses' Baxter found himself 'often' and 'suddenly relieved upon their prayers'.[3] He also succeeded in wrestling through the storm of his doubts. 'I was fain to dig to the very Foundations . . . that so my Faith might be indeed my own. And at last I found that Nothing is so firmly believed, as that which hath been sometime doubted of'; until 'Faith revived' and 'Man seemed nothing, and the World a shadow, and God was all'. The intertwining of a fearless use of his reason with his consuming sense of the presence of God, which is so marked a character in his personality, was already present; from the beginning he combined evident inspiration with an equally patent integrity. It is not surprising that he quickly won admiration and confidence, especially from young people. God 'toucht the hearts of young men and girles with a love of goodness and delightful obedience to the truth'; and in some cases, 'induced by their children', 'the Parents and

1. *Ibid.*, p. 2; and preface, fols. b3 verso, b4, c1 and c3: the two baptisms mentioned were both administered at Bridgnorth in 1640, one of them being of the bookseller Walter Kettilby (*101*, p. 168).
2. *114*, p. 226.
3. B. M. Egerton MS., 2570, fol. 7, from a passage omitted by Sylvester from *R.B.*, I, i, between §§37 and 38.

Grandfathers' also fell 'into liking and love of Piety'. Baxter 'took special notice of every one that was humbled, reformed or converted'; for 'I was wont to number them as Jewels'.[1]

In his eagerness and dogmatism—for about the things of which he was not in doubt Baxter always spoke downrightly—the young man also offended some, especially those to whom all his life he was content to refer as 'the ignorant Rout', 'the Rabble of the more vicious sort'. He offended them by his preaching. For 'telling them that Infants before Regeneration' were 'loathsome in the Eyes of God' (the violence of the phrase reflects his mental turmoil over baptising infants, but how could his hearers know this?) 'they railed at me as I passed through the Streets'. He offended them even more by his insistence on holiness of life and his desire for discipline. They tried to turn the tables: 'to feed their malice', they put it about that he had been seen consorting with a prostitute; and he was so ill advised as to take the case to court. Before long he found himself threatened with court proceedings.

In 1642 the Parliament ordered the defacing of all Images of any Person of the Trinity in Churches or Church-yards; [and] Because I read this Order and the Church-warden attempted to obey it, the rabble of drunken swearing Journeymen ... rose in a tumult with clubs, seeking to kill me and the Churchwardens.

I was walking almost a mile out of Town, or else I suppose I had there ended my days; [but] the Conforming Clergy were so much for them that one of them indicted me at the Assizes.[2]

In all these disturbances Baxter believed that he came off the victor, locally: 'the poor Sots were so amazed and ashamed, that they took on sorrily', 'they were ashamed and mute as fishes'. But it was not a promising beginning; and to be summoned to court was alarming, especially in days of incipient revolution, when 'a violent Country Gentleman seeing me pass the Streets, stopt and said, There goeth a Traitor', and when 'the Rabble' began crying 'Down with the Roundheads', 'and some they knockt down in the open Streets'.

In this Fury of the Rabble I was advised to withdraw a while from home; whereupon I went to Glocester: As I past but through a corner of the Suburbs of Worcester, they that knew me not, cried, Down with the Roundheads, and I was glad to spur on and be gone.

1. *96*, p. 1; *R.B.*, I, i, §§35f. and 136.
2. *101*, p. 158f.; *R.B.*, I, i, §56.

In Gloucester, where he was the guest of the Town Clerk, Baxter 'found a civil, courteous and religious People, as different from Worcester, as if they had lived under another Government'. Among them he met one who was to become 'my most faithful and familiar friend'[1] and for a time, thirty years later, to share his house, John Corbet, then Rector of St Mary de Crypt and usher to the Socinian John Bidle at the city corporation's school in that parish. Whether he also met Bidle Baxter does not say; probably not, since on another occasion he calls him simply 'one Mr Biddle, sometimes School-master in Glocester'.[2]

When, after a month at Gloucester, Baxter returned home, he found things not better but worse. 'The beggarly drunken Rowt' was now 'in a very tumultuating Disposition, ... like tyed Mastiffs newly loosed'. Furthermore, with the raising of the King's standard at Nottingham on 22 August, armies began to come abroad. 'I had neither Money nor Friends: I knew not who would receive me in any place of Safety': but 'I saw no safety in staying at home'. Baxter therefore again left Kidderminster, expecting soon to return; for 'we commonly supposed that a very few days or weeks by *one other* Battel, would end the Wars'. In the event he was away for nearly five years, at first living 'in quietness' at Coventry and later itinerating as a chaplain in the Parliamentarian army.

When recording his departure from Kidderminster, Baxter reveals no sense that his behaviour might be held to be cowardly or a dereliction of duty; nor did his enemies include this charge, when in later years they scoured his life for every possible reprehensible action. The ambiguous nature of his appointment, with its lack of any pastoral relationship, may have made it easier to break the ties so newly formed. Nor is it to be supposed that everyone else at Kidderminster stayed at home: 'when the Wars began, almost all these Drunkards went into the King's Army', and later Baxter had 'many score of my neighbours with me in the wars'.[3] To assess his action morally is perhaps possible only for those who have experienced the *sauve qui peut* fury of civil war, when in ethics, as in other fields, old and familiar landmarks are overturned or taken away altogether. Certainly Baxter's behaviour was neither worse nor better than that of many clergy. As a Parliamentarian

1. *105*, p. 27.
2. *R.B.*, I, i, §127.
3. *R.B.*, I, i, §59; D.W.L. MS., 4:126.

garrison Coventry became a city of refuge for a considerable number of ministers of a Puritan cast 'who fled thither for safety from Soldiers and Popular Fury, as I had done'. Most of these came out of Warwickshire or Leicestershire, but at least one besides Baxter was from Worcestershire, his friend Robert Morton. Nor were his companions in flight only ministers. 'When I was at Coventry the Religious part of my Neighbours at Kidderminster that would fain have lived quietly at home, were forced (the chiefest of them) to be gone: And to Coventry they came.'[1]

Although later Baxter sought to judge the issues between King and Parliament (which still divide us) more calmly and objectively, he confesses that 'I was then so zealous, that I thought it a great Sin for Men that were able to defend their Country, to be Neuters'; and it can hardly have been an open question for him, on which side he must stand.

I was always satisfied [he insists] that the Authority and Person of the King were inviolable [and] I never thought the Parliament blameless. [But] I favoured the Parliaments Cause, as they professed, I. To bring Delinquents to a Legal Trial: 2. And to preserve the Person and Government of the King by a Conjunction with his Parliament. . . . We that lived quietly in Coventry . . . were unfeignedly for King and Parliament.

In politics as in ecclesiastical matters Baxter constantly adhered to a 'moderate' position which from both sides would bring him charges of betrayal or insincerity; and in 1642 this position could not be accused of the *naïveté* which later it came to have. Ecclesiastically, Baxter explains how 'the Interest of the Diocesans and of the Prophane and Ignorant sort of People were unhappily twisted together', while not only 'all the Nonconformists' but 'others of the most serious godly People were alienated from' the bishops. 'Not that the Matter of Bishops or no Bishops was the main matter,' he adds; but the impeachment of the bishops was well understood and welcomed by 'the *generality* of the People through the Land (I say not *all*, or every one) who were then called Puritans' and was one reason 'why so great a number of men who were counted most Religious, fell in with the Parliament'.[2] Baxter's political hopes were to be disappointed, and he never ceased to condemn the execution of the King; but at the beginning

1. *R.B.*, I, i, §§61 (naming several ministers) and 63.
2. *R.B.*, I, i, §§55, 73 and 49; *106*, ii, p. 43.

of the war so convinced a Puritan could not do otherwise than side with the Parliament.

Before he settled in Coventry, Baxter was present at the first skirmish of the war on 23 September at Powick Bridge, near Worcester. 'I had a great mind to go see them, having never seen any part of an Army'; and although what he saw 'quickly told me the Vanity of Armies', he could not resist going a month later 'to see the Field where they had fought' at Edgehill. He had been preaching 'at Alcester for my Reverend Friend Mr Samuel Clark' (the friend whom twenty years later he would choose to marry him), and 'as I was preaching the People heard the Cannon play'. Next day both Clark and Baxter 'for curiosity went . . . to see the place, and the Relicts of the unburied slain: there were about a Thousand dead Bodies in the Field . . . two days after the fight'; but this was rather 'to go see whether two or three that of old had been my Intimate Friends in Cromwell's Army . . . were dead or alive'.[1]

In Coventry, after staying a month with the former schoolmaster at Bridgnorth, Simon King, now curate at Trinity Church, 'not paying them a penny for my diet', Baxter accepted an offer from 'the Committee and Governour of the City' to 'lodge in the Governour's House, and preach to the Soldiers'; and 'I lived in the Governours House, and followed my Studies as quietly as in a time of Peace, for about a year, only preaching once a week to the Soldiers, and once on the Lord's Day to the People, not taking of any of them a Penny for either, save my Diet only'. In his autobiography Baxter numbers it among his advantages at Kidder-minster that 'at first I was in the Vigour of my Spirits, and had naturally a familiar moving Voice (which is a great matter with the common Hearers)'; but in 1656 he wrote, 'I myself had once as naturally persuading and moving a voice as most men had, (others being judges;) and the great church at Coventry forcing me to raise it to the highest, did so deprive me of the command and familiar use of it, that it was quickly fixed in an ineffectual reading tone, which I never since could overcome.'[2] In the autumn of 1644 Baxter returned for two or three months to his native county, where at Wem he assisted in the establishment of the first Parliamen-tarian garrison in Shropshire and also 'redeemed my Father out of

1. *134*, p. 13; *R.B.*, I, i, §§60f. and 73.
2. *R.B.*, I, i, §§61 and 137 (2); *Autobiography of Henry Newcome* (*ut sup.*), ii, p. 343.

Prison' at Lilleshall Abbey. His father, who was soon in prison again at Shrewsbury, 'and all his Neighbours that were noted for praying and hearing Sermons', had first been 'plundered by the King's Soldiers, so that some of them had almost nothing but Lumber left in their Houses'. For himself, Baxter had 'nothing to lose, but Books and a Horse', but these 'were lost', save that 'part of my books were preserved'.[1]

After this excursion, Baxter returned to Coventry to his 'old Habitation and Imployment' for almost another year; and to the end of his life he counted it among God's mercies that he lived so long 'in safety in a City of defence, . . . seeing no enemy while the Kingdom was in Wars and Flames; and only hearing of the common Calamities round about,' 'as Men in a dry House do hear the Storms abroad. . . . And "do you hear the News?" was commonly the first Word I heard'.[2] To his 'dearly beloved friends, the inhabitants of the city of Coventry, both magistrates and people' he dedicated the third part of *The Saints Everlasting Rest*, 'in thankful acknowledgment of their great affection towards him, and ready acceptance of his labours amongst them'. He also presented a copy to the Mayor and Corporation of the city. Their letter of acknowledgement is still extant, though not the 'silver college cup, having the elephant (the city's arms) engraven thereon' which accompanied it as 'a small token of our affection to you', nor the book, which was 'ordered to be transferred yearly . . . from mayor to mayor'.[3] A letter preserved in the city's archives shows that Baxter later sent a copy of the second edition, but this also is not now to be found.[4] If a tradition recorded in 1820 is correct, he sometimes went outside the city to preach. A delightful story tells how, by saying that his employment was that of a 'man catcher', he persuaded a magistrate intent on arresting him to accompany him to the village of Berkswell and there prayed with such 'seriousness and fervour' that the magistrate 'was soon melted into tears'.[5]

In this secure and somewhat detached position Baxter remained till the summer of 1645. He then, with the approval of the other

1. *R.B.*, I, i, §64; *3* (3rd ed.), p. 378.
2. *114*, p. 225; *R.B.*, I, i, §67.
3. D.W.L. MS. 6:121, printed by Powicke, i, appendix 4, where for 'James' Bryan read 'Jarvis'; cf. *ibid.*, p. 68, n. 1.
4. Coventry Corporation MS. letters, 2:226; photostat at Dr Williams's Library.
5. *Congregational Magazine*, iii (1820), p. 397f.

ministers in the city and with the consent (given at first, though later withdrawn) of the Committee and Governor, left Coventry for a more active and arduous life in the Parliamentarian army, being invited 'by my much Honoured friend',[1] Edward Whalley, to serve as chaplain to the regiment which he commanded. 'I was loth to leave my Studies, and Friends, and Quietness at Coventry; . . . but I thought the Publick Good commanded me.' For the next year he shared in the life of the New Model Army and in the succession of triumphs which followed Naseby. Between July and December he was present at the engagement at Langport and at the capture of Bridgwater, Sherborne and Bristol, and later for three weeks at the siege of Exeter. During 'the extream winter' he was in Buckinghamshire, from March to May at Banbury, and after its capture at Worcester, till that too fell on 22 July. Although, in contrast with his 'Sedentary Life' at Coventry which left him 'weaker than ever I was before', he found that 'riding much in the Army did me more good than anything', he now thought it advisable to go to London 'about my health'. His physician, Sir Theodore Mayerne, 'Archiater' to the King, whom he had already consulted before leaving Coventry, now 'sent me to Tunbridge-Waters, where I staid three weeks'. It was probably during this period that he visited Boxley Abbey, near Maidstone, where 'it did me good', he liked to recall, 'to see upon the old Stone Wall in the Garden a Summer-house with this inscription in great golden Letters, that In that place Mr G. Sandys after his Travels over the World, retired himself for his Poetry and Contemplations'.[2] He then returned to his regiment, with which, in desultory activity in the Midlands, he spent the first part of the winter; but in February 1647 his health collapsed altogether and his days with the army were suddenly over. 'In a cold and snowy season', 'having taken cold with riding thin clothed in the Snow', he 'fell into such a bleeding as continued six days, with some fits of intermission', till he had lost 'a Gallon of Blood by the Nose'. When this occurred, he was 'among Strangers, and not knowing how to get home', being quartered on Sir John Coke of Melbourn Hall, Derbyshire. After three weeks there, 'without any Acquaintance, but my Servant, about me', he was for a further three weeks entertained 'with great

---

1. *3* (3rd ed.), preface, fol. cI verso. In 1654 Baxter dedicated his *Apology* to Whalley as one of 'those that Live in our Estimation and Affection'.

2. *98*, epistle to reader; Sandys had died two years earlier.

kindness' by Verney Noel of Kirkby Mallory, Leicestershire, and
then for three months 'with the greatest Care and Tenderness' by
Sir Thomas and Lady Rous of Rous Lench, Worcestershire. Lady
Rous was 'a godly, grave, understanding Woman', who, when a
little earlier Baxter had been quartered at Rous Lench, had 'entertained me not as a Soldier but a Friend'.[1] Now, as he gratefully
acknowledged in his dedication to her husband and herself of the
first part of *The Saints Everlasting Rest*, the part which 'was
written under your Roof': 'when you heard I was suddenly cast
into extream weakness, you sent into several Counties to seek me
in my quarters, and missing of me, sent again, to fetch me to your
house, where for many months I found a Hospital, a Physician, a
Nurse, and real Friends, and (which is more than all) daily and
importunate Prayers for my recovery.' The gracious black-and-
white Court at Rous Lench still stands and a tree in the garden is
known as 'Baxter's Tree'; but a portrait of Baxter which hung in
the house is no longer there.[2]

Baxter's purpose in serving with the army is worth dwelling on.
These were the years when revolution, in giving new freedom to
many who were orthodox as well as genuinely religious, also
released all manner of extravagance and fantasy, and when not only
uniformity in the Church but the Church's unity seemed to be
splintering chaotically. At Coventry, where a Separatist congregation is known to have existed as early as 1626, the Anabaptists (as
he always calls Baptists) 'got a seperated society' during Baxter's
time there, and 'an Ancient Minister of competent learning and
parts', Benjamin Cox, 'was sent from London to confirm them'.
Baxter had much dispute with Cox and also, at the request of the
Committee and Governor of Coventry, 'preached many Sermons
against separation . . . and Rebaptizing', though he declined to
publish them. 'A few poor townsmen only were carried away', 'the
Souldiers and the rest of the City' were 'kept sound from all infection'; and 'when the Court News-book told the World of the
Swarms of Anabaptists in our Armies, we thought it had been a
meer Lye'.[3]

1. *R.B.*, I, i, §§85f., 9 and 128 (cf. §157).
2. For a photograph of the Court, see *Victoria County History of
Worcestershire*, iii, p. 497; and for a photograph of the portrait, see
Powicke, i, frontispiece, with reproduction in Lloyd Thomas's abridgement of *R.B.*, facing p. 148.
3. *3* (3rd ed.), preface, fols. b4 verso and c1; *R.B.*, I, i, §§66 and 73.

When, however, Baxter visited 'the Armies Quarters before Leicester' after the battle of Naseby, he 'found a new face of things which I never dreamt of'. 'Cromwell's chief Favourites', who 'most honoured the Separatists, Anabaptists, and Antinomians, had got into the highest places . . . and by their very heat and activity bore down the rest'. It was to do his best to stem this fatal infection, as he believed it to be, that he accepted Whalley's offer of a chaplaincy.

From Naseby Fight I wholly laboured to have drawn off their souldiers from Errour, and Rebellion, and Usurpation.
I set myself from day to day . . . to discourse and dispute them out of their mistakes, both Religious and Political, [and] for those two years that I was among them, I found all friendly acceptance and respect, and never fell out with one man among them.

By his 'moving life', Baxter also 'had opportunity to preach in many Countreys and Parishes', and the congregations 'commonly seemed to be much affected'. He further took part on occasion in the public disputes on religious topics which were then a favourite and characteristic pastime. The Chiltern country, for instance, had many Baptists in it, as it still has; so, while quartered at Amersham, where 'some sectaries of Chesham had set up a Publick Meeting . . . I alone disputed against them from Morning until almost Night', till 'the Sectaries were so discouraged that they never met there any more'.[1]

With the leaders of the army, however, Baxter's efforts were fruitless. He was too late: the damage was done, and he 'reprehended' himself for not having accepted Cromwell's offer earlier of a chaplaincy with 'that famous Troop which he began his Army with', 'for then all the Fire was in one Spark'. Cromwell's 'Designs were visible' to Baxter: 'when a place fell void, it was Twenty to one a Sectary had it'. With growing uneasiness and disapproval Baxter observed how after Langport 'an Hundred Pounds Reward was voted to' Hugh Peter for bringing the news to London, 'and to Major Bethel for his Service, but none to Capt. Evanson, because he was no Sectary'; and how, 'two or three days before' the fall of Worcester, Whalley, who 'was called a Presbyterian', was displaced by Thomas Rainborow, 'that he might have the

1. *R.B.*, I, i, §§73, 77, 85 and 80; *106*, ii, p. 43; *3* (3rd ed.), preface, fol. c2. The original building and furnishings of the Amersham Baptist church (now disused) date, in fact, from the 1650s.

honour of taking the City', to 'gratifie the Sectaries'. Rainborow, who is now remembered and commended for his *mot* 'The poorest he hath a life to live as well as the richest he', was in sympathy with the Levellers; and in Baxter's opinion the links between the Levellers and the Anabaptists were not open to dispute.

We know the Masters of the Design to be Anabaptists of the highest form . . . and all the professing part of the Souldiery of my acquaintance were of the same way. . . . S. Georges Hill, and their printed Pamphlets shew whether they were for Community, or not.[1]

The reference here to St George's Hill, in Surrey, is a sidelong glance at Gerrard Winstanley and the Diggers, who, like the Baptists, were also strong in the Chiltern country where Baxter had served.

Over the moral and theological vagaries to which Anabaptism led, Baxter was still more troubled: 'Familism, Libertinism, and Paganism . . . all spring from the root of Anabaptistry,' he argued. The leader of the Ranters, for instance, Abiezer Coppe, 'now in Coventry Gaol' for blasphemy and 'filthy lascivious practices' 'was a zealous Anabaptist [and] re-baptized more than any one man that ever I heard of in the Countrey'; another Baptist, Paul Hobson, 'publisheth himself a Socinian to the world, teaching that God was never at enmity with men, but only men with God'; and 'I remember four years ago,' he wrote in 1650, 'when Anabaptistry had not been long in the Country, about Marsfield, and Trubridge, and those parts, they maintained that Christ took our sins into his nature, as well as our flesh'.[2] Apart from these excesses,

the most of them that I have known [Cox at Coventry among them], have made their Doctrine of Anabaptistry a ground of separation. . . . Oh how the Papists also are hardened by this! . . . and say to us, Now you may see what it is to depart from the unity, and bosom of the Church; [while] the Episcopal Party are far more confirmed in their way by it, and say, Now you see what it is to cut up the hedge, and pluck up the banks of Government.[3]

1. *3* (3rd ed.), p. 269.
2. *Ibid.*, p. 147f.; cf. the extract from a letter written by R(ichard) B(axter) to W(illiam) S(trong) from Withicomb (Withycombe Raleigh, Devon) on 27 October 1645, printed in Thomas Edwards, *Gangraena* (1646), I, ii, p. 1.
3. *Ibid.*, p. 144f.

To judge of a thing by 'what it leads to' is always open to the retort that 'it need not': Baxter did not abandon Puritanism because it led some into Anabaptistry, or cease to be a Protestant because some Protestants became Socinians; but that this analysis had truth and force in it is not open to doubt. Before the mounting political and religious radicalism—it is a common pattern in church history—Baxter's eager spirit was abashed, and he drew back. For the rest of his life he endeavoured passionately to inculcate the personal godliness and insistence on church discipline which made him a Puritan without allowing these to degenerate, or be dissipated, into Republicanism or Anabaptistry. When he returned to Kidderminster, his doubts over infant baptism were dispelled. A Nonconformist, unwillingly, he might one day have to be; a Sectarian, never.

Somewhat similarly, his unsympathetic assessment of Cromwell may be held to reflect prejudice. Cromwell's purpose, as well as his temperament, differed in many respects from Baxter's. Because, when they met at Leicester, Cromwell 'expostulated' with him for refusing the offer of a chaplaincy earlier,[1] he believed that Cromwell harboured a grudge against him. If, as Baxter asserts, Cromwell was 'acquainted the first day that I went into the Army . . . that I was sent . . . to try whether I could turn the Soldiers against his subverting Designs', it is not surprising that 'he would never once speak to me while I was in the Army' and 'would never let me once come near him or the Head-quarters'.[2] Nevertheless, his observation that the rise of the sects owed very much to Cromwell's patronage, like his delineation of the effect on Cromwell's character of 'Prosperity and Success', was shrewd and will not now be questioned.

If, during these years away from Kidderminster, Baxter's awareness of the perils of the day was sharpened, and with this of his duty to fight them, so also was his sense of pastoral responsibility. One thing that prompted him to enter the army was that 'many of my dearest friends were there, whose society had formerly been delightful to me, and whose welfare I was tender of, being men that had a deeper interest in my affections than any in the world

---

1. Who accepted the offer 'is uncertain': C. H. Firth, in Royal Historical Society *Transactions*, n.s., xiii (1899), p. 56.
2. *R.B.*, I, i, §74; *106*, ii, p. 203 (cf. *R.B.*, I, i, §76); *103*, pt iii, p. 102 (cf. *R.B.*, I, i, §82).

had before that time'; and 'it was they that stuck to me and I to them', he wrote in 1658. He resolved 'then in the wars that if ever God restored us, I would not forsake them, if now they forsook not him and me, . . . my faithful people, that purposely went with me (through so many years' wars and dangers and sufferings) to engage me not to leave them'.[1] The warmth of this passage may serve as an index of the feeling with which he will have read the forty-five names added in a distinct group, as 'The Souldiers', to the letter inviting him to return to Kidderminster; among them were two of the feoffees who had first approached him in 1641. That so many of his companions in the army had remained faithful not only to him but to God must have moved him still more; for he now had first-hand evidence of the temptations by which they had been beset. 'I am not at all so sharp against Wars and Souldiers as Erasmus was,' he could write in 1672, and, a year later, 'I am not simply against the lawfulness of War'; 'but it must be a very extraordinary Army, that is not constituted of Wolves and Tigers, and is not unto common honesty and piety, the same that a Stews or Whorehouse is to chastity', and 'O how hard is it to keep up a life of faith and godliness in an Army?' Although in 1647 he could write, 'O the sad and heart-piercing spectacles that mine eyes have seen in four years space! . . . scarce a moneth, scarce a week without the sight or noise of blood,' and in 1654, to Whalley, 'The best is, we now draw no bloud,' Baxter himself had never in fact seen anyone killed (other than 'a Welsh-man, that understood not English' whom he saw shot dead in the next field, when on his visit from Coventry to Shropshire in 1644). 'The greatest calamity of War is the perniciousness of it to mens souls,' he held; and on this account 'it must be a very clear and great necessity that can warrant a War'.[2]

1. *3* (3rd ed.), preface, fol. c1 verso; D.W.L. ms., 4:126.
2. *124*, p. 148; *71*, 2nd pag., p. 42f.; *2*, p. 123; *8*, epistle dedicatory to whole work; *106*, i, p. 3.

CHAPTER 3

The Reformed Pastor

THE soldiers were not alone in being eager to have Baxter back in Kidderminster. Altogether, 265 names were attached to the invitation to him to return, which is still preserved among his manuscripts.[1] It was not the first time that they had sought to recover him. He had been to see them 'with Joy' nearly a year before, after the siege of Worcester, and they then 'expected that I should return to them', but at that time his judgement was for staying on in the army, and the ministers in Coventry, whose advice he again sought, had 'all voted me to . . . leave Kidderminster yet longer'. In the meanwhile there had been a development. Since 1642 the Parliamentary Committee for Plundered Ministers, which had replaced the Committee for Scandalous Ministers, had been in the practice of sequestering livings held by clergy considered delinquent, sometimes appointing others to succeed them, sometimes not; and during Baxter's convalescence at Rous Lench the Kidderminster people had renewed their charges against the vicar, with the consequence that the living had been sequestered, the finances being left in the hands of 'divers of the Inhabitants', probably the feoffees chosen earlier by the vicar. 'Our place being now vacant' are the first words in the letter with which, therefore, Baxter's 'truly affectionate friends' now approached him. This time they invited him to be not simply their 'lecturer' but their 'minister'; and they promised to 'afford' him 'all due encouragement and assistance'.

No doubt to their surprise, Baxter 'flatly refused'. It was not that he did not intend to return. On the contrary, as he soon wrote to them, it was 'lest I should forestall my return to you, for whom I took myself reserved' that 'I durst not fix in any other congregation' 'in the time of my forced absence from you'.[2] But some combination of scruple, shrewdness and sympathy made him unwilling to approve the legality of parliamentary sequestration so far as to accept the questionable

1. D.W.L. MS., 1:213.　　　　　　2. 2, preface to whole work.

benefits gained by depriving another man of his living. 'I would take only the Lecture, which by his own Consent and Bond I held before'.

His sincerity is demonstrated by what followed. The parishioners at first 'sought to Mr Brumskill, and others, to accept the Place'; but Oliver Bromskill, who had been with Baxter at Coventry and continued in friendly correspondence with him, preferred the wealthier sequestration of Loughborough, Leicestershire. Soon after Baxter's return, still as Lecturer, the parishioners, nothing abashed by his refusal, secretly obtained an order from the Worcestershire representatives of the Committee for Plundered Ministers (Sir Thomas Rous was one of them) appointing him to the living. Later, perhaps partly to silence his scruples, they also obtained a certificate from the Westminster Assembly approving the appointment.[1] At first they dared not let him know what they had done; but when in 1651 before the battle of Worcester their homes were 'full of Soldiers', they brought him the documents for security. He thus learned of what had been done without his consent. He was, however, careful to let it make no visible difference to his position. The sequestered vicar not only received the £40 per annum legally due to him as a fifth of the living's value, but continued to live in the vicarage and also 'oft read the Common Prayer at Sir Ralph Clares', which could have been prevented 'if I would have used Magistrates'. Baxter remained content with 'a few top rooms of another mans House' (which still stands) in the High Street and with £80 or £90 per annum. At Mitton, similarly, Turner, the scandalous curate, was allowed to keep his £10 per annum and also to 'read the Common Prayer . . . once a day' to 'some of the Church of England';[2] most of the remaining money available was paid to the curate put by Baxter in Turner's place, Richard Sargeant.

Another reason for Baxter's unwillingness to accept the benefice was, almost certainly, the state of his health. At Rous Lench he was 'as it were, with one foot in the grave'. 'Other Physicians' besides Sir Theodore Mayerne 'gave me up as hopeless', and Dr George Bates, later 'Archiater' to Charles II, concurred by correspondence; only Baxter's stepmother, when 'the Report came . . . that I was dead', said, after retiring for secret prayer, 'He is

1. See *Baxter Treatises*, edited by R. Thomas, p. 5b.
2. *R.B.*, I, i, §128; *101*, p. 72; *100*, preface, fol. A2.

not dead, but shall live for farther Service.'[1] Even when he had
recovered sufficiently to return to Kidderminster, he 'did all under
languishing Weakness, being seldom an hour free from pain'; and
for many years after his return his 'Pains and Weaknesses' were
'double or fourfold to what I had before', with 'the same Symptoms
as most men have about Fourscore years of Age'. 'Do the utmost
you can to get a faithful Minister, when I am taken from you,'
he wrote to his parishioners in 1650. He then still believed his
body was 'hasting to the dust' and bequeathed them *The Saints
Everlasting Rest* as 'the legacy of a dying man'.[2] In 1647 he must
have felt it to be senseless as well as unseemly to accept preferment.

Baxter refers so often to his physical infirmities, and more than
once dwells on them at such length, that it is customary to call him a
hypochondriac. Some of his doctors in fact said he had 'the
Hypocondriack Melancholy'. But 'it is by dear experience that I
have learnt how little Physicians know', he wrote in 1672, 'having
passed through the tryal of above thirty of them on my own body
long ago . . .; and most that I got was but the ruine of my own
body'.[3] For his biographer to keep recurring to this ill health would
become tedious beyond endurance; yet it would be wrong not to
attempt to convey some sense of the 'very terrible' pains which
hampered him at every turn. 'My chief Troubles were incredible
Inflamations of Stomach, Bowels, Back, Sides, Head, Thighs, as if
I had been daily fill'd with wind: So that I never knew, heard, or
read of any man that had near so much.' His blood was like 'thin
Ink' and would never 'coagulate or cohere', and haemorrhages continued to 'shed abroad upon my Eyes, and Teeth, and Jaws, and
Joynts, so that I had scarce rest night or day'. In addition, for two
years he had 'a Disease in my Eyes almost incredible' till 'I had
almost lost my Eye'; also, it goes without saying, 'terrible
Toothach'. In 1658 he first 'suspected the Stone'; and from 1673
onwards 'the pain which before only tired my Reins, and tore my
Bowels, now also fell upon my Bladder, and scarce any part or
hour is free'.[4] In 1766 the stone from his bladder was 'to be seen at
the Museum at Montague-house'; but, although it was still there
in 1830, when one of his biographers described its size, colour and

---

1. *2*, epistle dedicatory to whole work; *R.B.*, I, i, §9 (cf. §85); *135*,
p. 188.
2. *R.B.*, I, i, §§130 and 9; *2*, preface to whole work.
3. *124*, p. 48; cf. *R.B.*, I, i, §9 ('Six and thirty Physicians').
4. *R.B.*, I, i, §§9 and 134; III, i, §311 and ii, §76.

shape, in 1925 the editor of his autobiography 'failed, after inquiries, to trace it'.[1]

For a man in constant, daily pain not to write it in as an inescapable part of the background of his memoirs would hardly be honest; and in Baxter's case other motives, interestingly interwoven, served to justify such detailed descriptions of his complaints. In the first place, he had 'a Mind that would fain know all'[2] and an interest in experimentation which did not exclude his body. He also, like George Herbert and many another country parson, 'was forced five or six years by the Peoples Necessity to practise Physick',[3] and he hoped that a diagnosis of his troubles and a description of effectual remedies would be of assistance to others. We thus learn that he had to walk 'hard with almost all my strength, an hour before Dinner, and an hour before Supper, till I sweat well', and, with the same end in view to keep close to 'a great Fire' and to take 'Beer as hot as my Throat will endure, drunk all at once'; that he benefited greatly from sage '1. Well boiled in the Wort in all my Beer: 2. Well boiled in my Gruel for every Mornings Breakfast'; and that he 'tried Cow's Milk, Goats Milk, Breast Milk, and lastly, Asses Milk,' but none of them agreed with him, till he heard that a Quaker 'did still milk their Sheep' and found that 'Sheeps Milk' brought him 'the greatest increase of my Ease, Strength and Flesh, of anything that ever I had tried'.[4]

He was not in doubt, however, that on some occasions he had been cured by prayer—'it hath been my own case more than . . . ten times', he wrote in 1650—and to this he believed it his duty to bear witness. A favourable example, for he describes it in at least three places, was when for three months he 'had a Tumor rose on one of the Tonsils or Almonds of my Throat, round like a pease', 'hard as a Bone, and about as big as a . . . small Button', which he 'too oft looked at in the Glass', fearing cancer. 'No Means altered it'; till, 'in obedience to my Conscience', while preaching about 'Mercies upon Prayer', 'I annexed some thankful mention of my own Experiences; and suddenly the Tumour vanished'. 'As I came out of the Pulpit, I put my Finger in my Mouth to feel it, but

1. *Biographical Collections* (1766), i, p. 142, n. i; W. Orme, *Life and Times of Richard Baxter* (1830), i, p. 498, n. 1; J. M. Lloyd Thomas, in his abridgement of *R.B.*, p. 295.
2. *114*, p. 88f.
3. *R.B.*, I, i, §135.
4. *R.B.*, I, i, §§9 and 134; III, i, §312.

could feel nothing': 'nor did I either swallow it down or spit it out,
nor knew what went with it to this Day'.[1]

'The greatest external Personal Affliction of all my Life', he says,
was 'the unavoidable loss of my time' which these infirmities
caused. Besides the two hours spent in exercise every day, Sunday
included—though 'I do it privately on that day, lest I tempt others
to sin'—he could not get himself up before seven o'clock and then
took more than an hour to dress; 'and after Supper I can seldom
Study'.[2] This sense of time continually wasted, coupled with his
expectation of imminent death, drove him not to despair or
resignation but to the husbandry of every moment available. This
alone made possible his extraordinary activity and literary output.
It colours and sharpens whatever he said or wrote.

> I Preach'd, as never sure to Preach again
> And as a dying man to dying men.

These words from the *Poetical Fragments* which he published in
1681, the only phrase of his to have reached *Familiar Quotations*,
evidently pleased Baxter himself, for he repeated them often. 'As a
dying man,' he writes in his autobiography, 'my Soul was the more
easily brought to Seriousness, and to preach as a dying Man to
dying Men.'[3] Two and a half years after he was restored to his
parishioners, when he dedicated *The Saints Everlasting Rest* to
them, he included 'ten directions' which he wrote down 'as the
words of a dying man'.[4] It may be well to summarise them (in his
own words, but with several omissions) as an index to his deepest
concerns, a programme of what he would carry out if only he
could. We will then return with him to Kidderminster, examine
the situation as he found it and inquire how far what here he
characteristically puts into imperatives was, in fact, achieved.

1. Labor to be men of knowledg and sound understandings, let the
   Bible be much in your hands and hearts: Remember what I taught
   you on Deut.6: 6,7.
2. Do the utmost you can to get a faithful Minister, when I am taken
   from you; submit to his private Over-sight, as well as publike
   Teaching. It is but the least part of a Ministers work, which is done
   in the Pulpit.

1. 2 (10th ed.), p. 250 margin; *R.B.*, I, i, §130; *135*, p. 189f.
2. *R.B.*, I, i, §135; *62*, p. 137.
3. *98*, p. 40; *R.B.*, I, i, §137 (2); cf. §32, also *114*, p. 223.
4. *3* (3rd ed.), p. 272.

3. Let all your Knowledg turn into Affection and Practice; keep open the passage between your heads, and your hearts, that every Truth may go to the quick.

4. Be sure you make conscience of the great Duties that you are to perform in your families. If you cannot do what you should, yet do what you can.

5. Beware of extreams in the controverted points of Religion. As for separation, the mischief of it lies not in the bare error of judgment, but in the un-christian and church-dissolving division and alienation which thence followeth.

6. Above all, see that you be followers of Peace and Unitie, both in the Church, and among your selves. Remember what I taught you on Heb.12.14.[1] Those that say, No Truth must be concealed for Peace, have usually as little of the one, as the other. I ever loved a godly, peaceable Conformist, better then a turbulent Non-Conformist. I here charge you, That if God should give me up to any factious Church-rending course (against which I daily pray) that you forsake me, and follow me not a step. If any heart-burnings arise, do not keep strange, but go together, and lovingly debate it, or pray together, that God would reconcile you; O remember that piercing example of Christ, who washed his Disciples feet, to teach us that we must stoop as low to one another.

7. Above all, be sure you get down the pride of your hearts. Forget not all the Sermons I preached to you against this sin. No sin more natural, more common, or more deadly.

8. Be sure you keep the mastery over your flesh and senses. Few ever fall from God, but flesh-pleasing is the cause.

9. Make conscience of the great duty of reproving, and exhorting those about you: Admonish them lovingly and modestly, but be sure you do it, and that seriously.

10. Lastly, Be sure to maintain a constant delight in God, and a seriousness and spirituality in all his Worship. Think it not enough to delight in Duties, if you delight not in God. You are never stable Christians till you reach this. Never forget all those Sermons I preached to you on Psalm 37.4. Fear the beginnings and appearances of sin. Beware lest Conscience once lose its tenderness.

A copy of the second edition of the book which carries these 'ten directions' Baxter presented to his people, inscribed in his own hand, with the desire that it 'may be still in the custodye of the high Bayliff'; and it is 'carefully preserved in the Mayor's Parlour'[2] at Kidderminster. It is only one of the Baxteriana there. Apart from the statue of Baxter in the market-place, which was unveiled in 1875, his chair is preserved in the parish church, his communion

1. For this sermon, see *Baxter Treatises*, edited by R. Thomas, p. 28b, whence it should be transferred to section 1.

2. Powicke, i, p. 68, n. 1.

table in the Congregational church (called by his name, as is one
of the wards of the town), and his pulpit (refurbished and restored
to use in 1962) in the Unitarian church. This distribution of objects
associated with him, which is symbolic of the claim upon him by
differing communions and types of piety, is an ironic comment on
his desire to preserve unity at all costs; but it leaves no doubt of the
respect in which his memory is held at Kidderminster. The fact
that this is so, and the notable success which he had in transform-
ing the life of the town, must not lead us to forget that it was a
transformation or to suppose that his success was total. In course of
time a considerable number of his 'dearest people', 'of whose
welfare', he wrote in 1650, 'I am as tender as if they were my
children', came to return his affection and to respond to his over-
sight, so that he rejoiced in them as 'a people so willing to obey'.[1]
But this was never true of more than a proportion of them, and he
takes care not to claim that it was.

He describes the parish, which included part of the town of
Bewdley (then a chapelry in the parish of Ribbesford), as 'a Market
Town with twenty Villages', 'near 20 miles about', consisting of
'about three or four thousand souls' or 'eight hundred Families',
'1800 or more of which were at age to be Communicants'. Of these,
'all refused to do any more than hear me preach, (for fear of
discipline) except about 600 or a few more'; while, if we are concerned only with 'such as the vulgar call precise, that are rated to
be serious Professours of Religion, (or perhaps somewhat more)',
the number would have to be reduced to 'about five hundred', i.e.
less than a third of the adult population and less than one per
family. Among the rest were 'some Papists', 'but few', and 'one or
two . . . turned Anabaptists'; some who, on the basis of a mis-
understanding of the doctrine of predestination or because they
were 'infected by the Infidels (who are all for Hobs [Hobbes] his
Necessity)', 'will not so much as promise Reformation' and others,
'but very few', 'of more plausible lives', who yet 'make it their
work to possess people with a hatred of strict Professours'; some
'secret Heathens' and others who patently 'know not almost any
more, then the veryest Heathen in America'—one 'thought Christ
was the Sunne . . . and the Holy Ghost was the Moone', 'and when
I repeat the History of the Incarnation, life, death, and resurrection

---

1. *3* (3rd ed.), p. 272 and preface, fol.d 3; *R.B.*, I, i, §137 (11) and (25);
2, epistle dedicatory to whole work.

of Christ to them, they stand wondering, and say, they never heard it before'; and lastly many who 'live in some notorious, scandalous sins',[1] especially drunkenness.

The drunkenness in Kidderminster, 'that Sin of which we were in most danger', caused Baxter constant grief. 'Above all,' he wrote in 1657, when he dedicated *A Treatise of Conversion* to the inhabitants of the town, 'it is the odious swinish sin of tipling and drunkenness, and suchlike sensuality, that declareth too many of you to be yet strangers to conversion'. 'The drunkards of above 12 or 20 if not 30 yeares standing are allmost weekly raging before my doores.' Yet even these drunkards who lived nearly next door to him he came to regard as indirectly assisting his labours, in that they were 'so beastly and ridiculous, that they made that Sin . . . the more abhorred'. It was also an advantage, and with his ruthless objectivity he recognised it as one, that 'most of the bitter Enemies of Godliness in the Town, that rose in Tumults against me before, . . . had gone out into the Wars, into the King's Armies, and were quickly kill'd'.[2]

Whatever its faults, and he is frank in categorising them, Baxter held Kidderminster to be 'as honest a Town as any I know in England', admitting that he did not know another parish 'in England of so much Godliness, and tractableness'. Looking back in later years, he recalled as 'a great Advantage' the 'holy, humble, blameless Lives of the Religious sort', and 'the Zeal and Diligence of the Godly People of the Place'. 'The Town liveth upon the Weaving of Kidderminster Stuffs; and as they stand in their Loom they can set a Book before them, or edifie one another.' This was the not unpromising material already there for him to work upon; but there can be no doubt of the transformation which he effected. 'When I came thither first, there was about one Family in a Street that worshipped God and called on his Name'; 'when I came away there were some Streets where there was not past one Family in the Side of a Street that did not so'. 'On the Lord's Days there was no disorder to be seen in the Streets, but you might hear an hundred Families singing Psalms and repeating Sermons, as you passed through the Streets'; and 'those People that had none in their Families who could pray, or repeat the Sermons, went to their

1. *100*, pt ii, pp. 9 and 185; *29*, pp. 157–65.
2. *R.B.*, I, i, §137 (3) and (22); D.W.L. MS., item 352 in *Baxter Treatises*, edited by R. Thomas, p. 26a; *29*, *loc. cit.*

next Neighbour's House who could do it, and joined with them'.[1]

Baxter always urges whatever matter is his present subject with such vehemence that for the time, forgetting what he has written elsewhere, one is tempted to suppose that this is what he cared about most. But no one then or now could think that because, when commending pastoral oversight, he wrote 'it is but the least part of a Ministers work, which is done in the Pulpit', he did not think preaching 'the most excellent'[2] part, calling for all that a man has.

It is a fearful case [he writes] to be an unsanctified Professor, but much more to be an unsanctified Preacher.

Preach to your selves the Sermons that you study, before you preach them to others; [for] God never saved any man for being a Preacher; [and] many a Preacher is now in hell.

All the week long is little enough to study how to speak two hours.

Be much, above all, in secret prayer and meditation: [the people] will likely feel when you have been much with God.

In preaching, there is intended a communion of souls, and a communication of somewhat from ours unto theirs.

[Then] see that you have a constant seriousness; ... especially see that there be no affectation; ... remember that they must be wakened or damned.

These are but a few of the forceful exhortations scattered through a work mainly concerned with matters other than preaching, *The Reformed Pastor*. They reflect unmistakably what Baxter himself sought to do, and to be, as a preacher with evangelical passion. 'I was to preach, not onely to a popular Auditory, but to the most ignorant, sottish part of that Auditory.' He drew on his memories of the days

when God first warmed my heart with these matters, and when I was newly entered into a Seriousness in Religion: when I read such a book as Bishop Andrews *Sermons*, or heard such kind of preaching, I felt no life in it: methoughts they did but play with holy things.... But it was the plain and pressing downright Preacher, that onely seemed to me to be in good sadness, and to make somewhat of it, and to speak with life, and light, and weight.[3]

For himself, he was 'very sensible that I have not reached the thing that I desired; ... that there wanteth that life and piercing

1. *29*, *loc. cit.*; *R.B.*, I, i, §§136 and 137, (6), (7) and (15).
2. *17*, p. 78.
3. *20*, epistle to reader.

quickness, which may concur with plainness'. 'I seldom come out
of the Pulpit, but my Conscience smiteth me that I have been no
more serious and fervent. . . . It asketh me, ". . . Shouldst thou not
weep over such a people, and should not thy tears interrupt thy
words?" '[1]—as, we may recall, they did on one of his visits to
Bridgnorth. One hopes that his conscience was quietened a little
by the effect of his preaching. He acknowledges that he had 'an
attentive diligent Auditory': 'the Congregation was usually full,
so that we were fain to build five Galleries'.[2] What Matthew
Sylvester, who knew him only in extreme old age, says of Baxter's
speaking in general may be taken to be peculiarly applicable
to his way of preaching. 'He had a moving πάθος, and useful
Acrimony in his words; neither did his Expressions want their
Emphatical Accent, as the Matter did require. And when he spake
of weighty Soul-Concerns, you might find his very Spirit Drench'd
therein.'[3] Edmund Calamy's description of him, from within a few
months of his death, is strikingly similar: 'He talked in the pulpit
with great freedom about another world, like one that had been
there, and was come as a sort of an express from thence to make a
report concerning it.'[4]

The reference a little earlier to preaching for two hours is to the
two services on Sundays, not to one. 'I preached before the Wars
twice each Lord's Day; but after the War but once', the assistant,
who preached at Mitton 'one half the day', preaching 'in the town
the other'. Baxter's health did not permit him to preach more than
once a Sunday: 'I can hardly on any Lords day speak above an
hour without the prostration of my strength, and extream languishing of my body.' He was also prone to catch cold in the unheated
church. 'I lately preached against sitting at prayer,' he writes in
January 1657, and 'for the comeliness of being uncovered all the
time of God's worship . . . (and when I had done, though I wore
fivefold of caps on my head, I took a dangerous cold, and was fain
to use my hat again when I hear, though when I am speaking I feel
no great miss of it).'[5]

F. J. Powicke suggests that 'the swiftness and preparedness'

1. *Ibid.*; *17*, p. 370.   2. *R.B.*, I, i, §136.
3. M. Sylvester, *Elisha's Cry after Elijah's God* (in *R.B.*, *ad cal.*), p. 14.
4. E. Calamy, *Historical Account of my Own Life*, edited by J. T. Rutt
(1829), i, p. 220f.
5. *R.B.*, I, i, §§135 and 137 (11); *3* (3rd ed.), preface, fol. d1 verso;
D.W.L. MS., 1:129.

with which in 1661 Baxter composed *The Reformed Liturgy* within a fortnight may be accounted for 'by the fact that he was but writing out and supplementing what he had practised at Kidderminster'.[1] Of the order of service this may be true, in whole or in part; but in so far as *The Reformed Liturgy* is, as the name indicates, a reforming of the 'liturgy' of the Book of Common Prayer, it is incorrect. In a letter of 1658 Baxter describes his practice thus:

As to the report of my using a form, the truth is, I never used one publicly or privately since I was 17 or 18 years of age; except the Lord's Prayer, which I use most Lord's Days once; . . . and except that I used much of the public liturgy in the congregation the first year and half of my ministry. And I find myself of late disposed in secret to end with the Lord's Prayer, as having a perfect method and satisfactory comprehensiveness of all that I had omitted.[2]

In 1684 it was still his practice to pray 'without a form', but only because for himself this was 'so much easier' than 'to remember a form of words'.[3] 'For my own part,' he says elsewhere, 'it is easier to me to pray or preach six hours in freedome, about things which I understand, than to pray or preach the tenth part of an hour in the fetters of a form of words which I must not vary'.[4]

Yet, in general, and objectively, he was in no way opposed to the use of forms. In *A Christian Directory* he sensibly and characteristically ends a comparison of 'the Commodities and Incommodities' of 'set Forms of Words' and 'free praying without them' by recommending 'somewhat of both wayes joyned together'.[5] Forms of prayer of his own composition for those at different stages of Christian maturity are scattered through his writings. These were intended as 'a help subordinate to the Spirits help, to those that have it but in part; as Spectacles to dark Sights, and Sermon Notes to weak Memories; . . . I can truly say, that Forms are oft a help to me'.[6] This may imply that he used notes to assist him in public prayer, as we know he did in preaching: 'I use notes as much as any man, when I take pains,' he once retorted to a Quaker critic; 'and as little as any man, when I am lazy, or busie, or have not leisure to prepare.'[7] Powicke's suggestion is probably so far correct that regular practice in the composition of prayers

1. Powicke, i, p. 95.
2. D.W.L. MS., 5:9.
3. *118*, 'Account', p. 20.
4. *71*, 1st pag., p. 852.
5. *Ibid.*
6. *118*, 'Account', p. 19.
7. *15*, p. 20.

seems as much implied by the quality of *The Reformed Liturgy* as by the speed with which it was produced. 'Baxter's diction excels,' a modern student of liturgy has written of this work, 'in the combination of economy of language, sustained dignity and directness'; 'no formal wording could have the arrow-like directness'[1] of the Exhortation in Baxter's Communion Order. On this Baxter's own sober comment would have been, 'Words must be used and weighed; but the main work is heart work.'[2]

If his responsibility for his people's souls made Sunday a day of dreadful solemnity, it was also a day of special gladness for Baxter, bringing him 'happy opportunity' for delight in God. His constant recurrence to this theme does much to relieve the conventional picture of the gloomy Puritan and his way of worship.

If anything on Earth be like to Heaven, it is to have our Delight in God. And therefore if anything may make us Heavenly, it is that which raiseth us to such delights. And therefore a Chore of holy persons, melodiously singing the Praises of Jehovah, are likest to the Angelical Society. Psalm 150.[3]

The psalm-singing to be heard in the people's homes on Sundays was in response to Baxter's appeal not only to ministers but to 'all Christs Redeemed ones' to 'spend more of those days in Praise and Thanksgiving, especially in Commemoration of the whole work of Redemption (and not of Christs Resurrection alone)', and to do it 'with the most heart-raising cheerfulness and melody; especially in the holy assemblies'.

The Lords day is a day of Joy and Thanksgiving, and the Praises of God are the highest and holyest employment upon Earth. And if ever you should do any thing with all your might, and with a joyful and triumphing frame of soul, it is this.

The thankful and praiseful Commemoration of the work of mans Redemption, is the special work of the day: and the celebrating of the Sacrament of the body and blood of Christ, (which is therefore called the Eucharist) was part of these laudatory exercises and used every Lords day by the Primitive Church. . . .

For myself [Baxter says] I confess that Harmony and Melody are the pleasure and elevation of my Soul, and have made a Psalm of Praise in the holy Assembly the chief delightful Exercise of my Religion and my Life.[4]

1. Horton Davies, *The Worship of the English Puritans* (1948), p. 159.
2. *118*, 'Account', p. 21.
3. *71*, pt iii, p. 167.
4. *6*, p. 533; *71*, 1st pag., pp. 176 and 757; *98*, epistle to reader.

In Baxter's 'weak judgement', 'it would be no sinful humane Invention or addition' 'if Hymns and Psalms of Praise were new invented, as fit for the state of the Gospel, Church and Worship, . . . as Davids Psalms were fitted to the former state and infancy of the Church'. 'Sure there is somewhat of Heaven in Holy Poetry'. He would rejoice, we may suppose, that verses from the *Poetical Fragments* 'written in various Passions', which he published in 1681, are now sung by Christians of many communions. More conventional Puritan scruples, however, strictly limiting worship to what could be justified from Scripture, then still excluded all forms of praise but the Psalms.

> I could wish [Baxter wrote in 1653] that the Ministers of England . . . would unanimously agree on some one Translation of the English Psalms in meeter, better then that in common use, and if it may be, better then any yet extant (not neglecting the poëtical sweetness under pretence of exact translating) or at least to agree on the best now extant: (the London Ministers may do well to lead the way).[1]

A year later the ministers in the recently formed Worcestershire Association duly sent a letter, signed first by Baxter, to the ministers in the London Provincial Assembly, asking them to do this. 'Of all the versions that yet we have seen', the Worcestershire ministers were in doubt which of two 'accurate and desirable' versions was preferable: Francis Rous's *Psalmes of David*, which was 'close to the text' and had the advantage of approval by the Westminster Assembly and adoption by the Church of Scotland, or 'that of Mr William Barton's now in the press (some of which we have seen)'.[2] The London ministers' reply[3] was ineffectual, and in *The Reformed Liturgy* Baxter still commends these two versions as 'the best that we have seen' and pleads for them both '(for grateful variety) to be printed together on several columns or pages'. We may perhaps assume that the version used at Kidderminster was that of Barton, with whom Baxter is known to have been in correspondence. 'It was at Baxter's request that he made four metrical renderings of the Te Deum';[4] and to the 1670 edition of Barton's *Centuries of Select Hymns* Baxter contributed a commendatory epistle.

For Baxter all public worship, whether preaching, prayer or

1. *6*, p. 534f.
2. D.W.L. MS., 1:246.
3. *Ibid.*, 2:279.
4. *Dictionary of Hymnology*, edited by J. Julian, *s.v.* Barton.

praise, was to be informed with an intense devotion. In his *Divine Appointment of the Lords Day* we find this exhortation:

Preach with such life and awakening seriousness; Preach with such grateful holy eloquence, and with such easie method, and with such variety of wholesome matter, that the people may never be aweary of you . . . Pray with that Heavenly life and fervour as may wrap up the souls of those that joyne with you, and try then whether they will be aweary: Praise God with that joyful alacrity which beseemeth one that is ready to pass into Glory, and try whether this will not Cure the peoples weariness.[1]

The manner of observing the sacraments at Kidderminster is recorded in a letter written by Baxter in March 1657. His description of the Lord's Supper is as follows:

A long table being spread, I first open the nature and use of the ordinance, and the qualification and present duty of the communicants; and then the deacons (3 or 4 grave, pious men chosen and appointed to that office) do set the bread and wine on the table; and in prayer we beseech the Lord to accept of those his own creatures now dedicated and set apart for his service, as sanctified to represent the body and blood of his Son; and after confession of sin, and thanksgiving for redemption, with commemoration of the sufferings of Christ therein, and ransom thereby, we beg the pardon of sin, and the acceptance of our persons and thanksgivings now offered up to God again, and his grace to help our faith, repentance, love, etc. and renewal of our covenant with him, etc. And so after the words of institution etc. I break the bread, and deliver it in Christ's general terms to all present, first partaking myself, and so by the cup: which is moved down to the end of the table by the people and deacons (who fill the cup when it is emptied); and immediately after it, each one layeth down his alms to the poor, and so arise, and the next tableful succeedeth to the last: after which I first proceed to some words of exhortation, and then of praise and prayer, and sing a psalm, and so conclude with the blessing.[2]

It is of interest to compare this Order with 'the Order of celebrating the Sacrament of the Body and Blood of Christ' in *The Reformed Liturgy*, the doctrine of which, Professor Ratcliff has recently observed, 'is markedly higher than the doctrine expressed or implied in the Communion Office of the Prayer Book of 1552 or 1559', 'Baxter's conception of the liturgical action' being 'nearer to the historic western tradition than the conception which Cranmer embodied in the Communion Service of the Prayer

1. *62*, p. 124.
2. D.W.L. MS., 3:156.

Book of 1552'.[1] The two Orders are similar but not identical. In particular, the thanksgiving which Professor Ratcliff finds curiously absent from the Order in *The Reformed Liturgy* was not lacking in the Order observed at Kidderminster.

In *The Reformed Liturgy* Baxter pleads that 'none of the people be forced to sit, stand, or kneel, in the act of receiving, whose judgment is against it'. At Kidderminster, as we know from a sermon of 1657, 'all here receive the sacrament sitting'; but the charge that 'ever I refused one person meerly because they would take it kneeling'[2] Baxter repudiates as slander. He had in fact invited Sir Ralph Clare 'to the Sacrament, and offered it him kneeling', but Sir Ralph and those of his mind 'would not come, unless I would administer it to him and his Party on a day by themselves, when the rest were not present',[3] and this Baxter would not do. While allowing many cases 'such as may admit a dispensation', the sacraments were normally to be administered in public. 'It's the whole church that must come together to that end ordinarily.'[4]

Those who assisted in the administration at Kidderminster Baxter was careful, as we have seen, to term deacons, not elders. 'I have written these 35 years against Lay-Elders,'[5] he wrote in 1682, and he was far from thinking their presence obligatory in the observance of the Lord's Supper. To a minister in Shrewsbury, who could not persuade any of his parishioners to become elders and who was told 'In another place you might administer the sacraments without elders, but not in Shrewsbury', Baxter wrote sharply, 'It is not the work of a classis or any church governors to judge whether God should be worshipped in his ordinances or not.'[6]

The sermon of 1657 mentioned above was preached on Christmas Eve. 'Tomorrow,' he observes in it, 'is the day called Christmass day, and many days called Holy days do follow it.' 'There is no proof that ever I saw,' he remarks, 'that the Church observed any of these days, of many hundred years after Christ.'[7] 'I am satisfied,' he writes elsewhere, 'that it is impossible to know

1. E. C. Ratcliff, in *From Uniformity to Unity 1662–1962*, edited by G. F. Nuttall and O. Chadwick (1962), p. 123.
2. *39*, p. 364.
3. *R.B.*, I, ii, §154.
4. D.W.L. MS., 3:102.
5. *106*, ii, p. 66.
6. D.W.L. MS., 1:253, dated 12 November 1656 *natali Authoris*.
7. *39*, pp. 365 and 367.

the day of Christ's nativity.'[1] Christmas, therefore, he did not observe. On Easter Day, on the other hand, 'in these parts we never omit the administration of the Lord's Supper (in most of our congregations)'.[2]

The Order of baptism used at Kidderminster Baxter describes thus:

After the opening of the nature and use of the ordinance, I require the parents (both, where they can come) to profess their own faith, by owning the common creed when I have recited it, and by expressing that they take the Lord for their God and Christ for their Redeemer, and the Holy Ghost for their Sanctifier. And then I demand whether they desire this child to be baptized into this faith, and entered into this covenant with God the Father, Son and Holy Ghost (renouncing the world, the flesh and the devil). And after engaging them to a careful education of it, and prayer for God's acceptance of the child to be devoted to him, and blessing of the ordinance, etc. I baptize it and conclude with thanksgiving and prayer.[3]

The reference to reciting the creed will be noted. 'In all our Countrey, and where I came,' Baxter wrote later, 'I remember no Churches that did not use the Creed openly at their baptizing any, and the Decalogue frequently read out of *Exod*. 20. or *Deut*. 5. and the Lords prayer frequently; as we did constantly. But some thought that we were not bound to use it every time we prayed.'[4] The repeated use of all three elements in worship thus lies behind his reference to them in his autobiography as 'the most acceptable and plentiful matter, for all my Meditations: They are to me as my daily Bread and Drink'.[5]

During Baxter's years in Kidderminster men's minds were exercised, and much controversy was aroused, over the right subjects for admission to the Lord's Supper and for the baptism of their infant children. Men of Puritan sentiments were very largely agreed in being dissatisfied with the admission of all parishioners who, after (or even without) a formal teaching of 'the Words of the Catechism in the Liturgy',[6] had received episcopal confirmation, whatever their ignorance in fact of the Christian faith and however scandalous their lives. They found it much

1. D.W.L. MS., 3:156.
2. *Ibid.*, 6:221.
3. *Ibid.*, 3:156.
4. *106*, ii, p. 87.
5. *R.B.*, I, i, §213 (3).
6. *R.B.*, I, ii, §40.

harder to agree on the conditions for admission to be required: how far these should be only dogmatic or also ethical, what minimum amount of knowledge or morals must be demanded, and how either a genuine understanding or sincerity of life were to be judged. At what point were evil livers to be suspended from admission to the Lord's Table? Was baptism to be refused to the infants of those suspended and, equally, of those who absented themselves from the Lord's Supper? 'Many took up the way of Separation, and gathered Churches . . . according to their several opinions, because the Parishes were so bad, that they thought them uncapable of Discipline.'[1]

Letters seeking advice came to Baxter from many correspondents to whom separation was abhorrent, yet who almost despaired of the condition of their parishioners. 'Sir,' wrote a Wiltshire minister, 'the greater part of my poor people that will have their children baptized hate instruction and are as ignorant of Christianity, I mean of the plainest principles . . . as if they had never heard of them. I did not think rational creatures subject to so gross and affected ignorance. . . . And unless I will baptize them in all haste, away they run to some idle drunken fellows and think all well.' 'Upon examination,' wrote another who had returned from New England to Essex, 'I found the parents as ignorant or scandalous as heathens . . . I could find as good among our Indians. Now, Sir, to give the seal of the covenant by virtue of such I could not do it, conscience would fly in my face.' The same correspondent informed Baxter that the eminent Presbyterian Stephen Marshall was 'unsatisfied in the parochial way as now we stand, to baptize all, yet refuse above half at the Lord's Supper'—though Marshall, he added, was now 'out of the snare, being only a lecturer'. Others equally sincere were drawn to be less strict: they were 'fearful of putting the veriest weakling in Christianity by'.[2]

Baxter 'sifted this Point' of 'the Necessary Qualification and Title of Church-Members and Communicants'—'more exactly and diligently . . .', he says, 'than almost any Controversie whatsoever'. He then published *Certain Disputations of Right to Sacraments*. The book's purport was that 'it is not the reality of a

1. *100*, pt ii, p. 186.
2. D.W.L. MSS., 4:245; 3:104; 4:284: in 1651 Marshall left Finchingfield, Essex, where 'for seven years he had no administration of the communion' (*Dictionary of National Biography*), to become Town Preacher at Ipswich.

Dogmatical . . . Faith, nor yet the Profession of bare Assent . . .;
but only the Profession of a Saving Faith, which is the Condition
of Mens Title to Church-Communion *Coram Ecclesiâ*'.[1] His argument gained strength from his unshakable assurance that 'there
would not be many found notoriously ungodly amongst our
people', if only ministers would give themselves unstintingly to
the task of 'Personal Conference with every Family apart, and
Catechizing and Instructing them'.[2] To these weekday activities
among his own parishioners we now turn. They were at once the
presupposition and the justification of the measures of discipline
which he introduced at Kidderminster, and which must also be
briefly described. Catechizing and discipline together were, moreover, the basis for the Association of ministers which he formed in
Worcestershire and which became a model for many other counties
throughout the country.

'It is but the least part of a Ministers work, which is done in the
Pulpit', he stated roundly in his 'ten exhortations' to his people in
1650; and 'of all the Works that ever I attempted', he wrote looking back, 'this'—'personal Conference with every one about the
State of their own Souls, together with Catechizing'—'yielded me
most Comfort in the practice of it'. Nor was 'with every one' an
easy exaggeration. 'Except three or four Families that refused to
come to me, (whom yet I knew by other means) I knew not only
the persons but the measures of all or almost all their understandings in the Town, and my assistants in the Villages knew the rest,
by personal conference, each family coming to us by turns.'[3] It will
be of interest to set down in some detail the course followed.

I set two Days a Week apart for this Employment: my (faithful
unwearied) Assistant and my self, took fourteen Families every Week;
those in the Town came to us in our Houses. . .; those in the Parish my
Assistant went to, to their Houses: First they recited the Catechism to
us (a Family only being present at a time, and no Stranger admitted);
after that I first helpt them to understand it, and next enquired modestly
into the State of their Souls, and lastly, endeavoured to set all home to
the convincing, awakening and resolving of their Hearts according to
their several Conditions; bestowing about an Hour (and the Labour of
a Sermon) with every Family. [And] though the first time they came with

1. *R.B.*, I, i, §171.
2. *18*, p. 251; *R.B.*, I, i, §137 (24).
3. *2*, epistle dedicatory to whole work; *R.B.*, I, ii, §40f.; *100*, pt ii, p. 9
(cf. *R.B.*, *loc. cit.*: 'except half a dozen . . . Families').

Fear and Backwardness, after that they longed for their turn to come again.[1]

Few Families went from me without some tears, or seemingly serious promises for a Godly Life. . . . If any of them were stalled through Ignorance or Bashfulness, I forbore to press them any farther to Answers, but made them Hearers, and either examined others, or turned all into Instruction and Exhortation. . . . All the Afternoons on Mondays and Tuesdays I spent in this: [and] my Assistant spent the Mornings of the same Days in the same Employment.[2]

'The clerk goeth a week before to every family,' Baxter wrote at the time, 'to tell them when to come, and at what hour (one family at eight o'clock, the next at nine, and the next at ten, etc.).'[3]

These 'private Conferences with the families' Baxter found so taxing that (except for his writing) all his other labours seemed in comparison 'as it were the work of my spare hours'. In addition, after the weekly 'lecture' on Thursdays for which he had first come to the parish,

Every Thursday Evening my Neighbours that were most desirous and had Opportunity, met at my House, and there one of them repeated the Sermon, and afterwards they proposed what Doubts any of them had about the Sermon, or any other Case of Conscience, and I resolved their Doubts: And last of all I caused sometimes one, and sometimes another of them to Pray (to exercise them); and sometimes I prayed with them my self: which (beside singing a Psalm) was all they did. And once a Week also some of the younger sort who were not fit to pray in so great an Assembly, met among a few more privately, where they spent three Hours in Prayer together. Every Saturday Night they met at some of their Houses to repeat the Sermon of the last Lord's Day, and to pray and prepare themselves for the following Day.[4]

These private meetings also

were a marvellous help to the propagating of Godliness among them: for thereby Truths that slipt away were recalled, and the Seriousness of the Peoples minds renewed; and good desires cherished; and hereby their knowledge was much increased; and here the younger sort learned to pray, by frequent hearing others: And here I had opportunity to know their Case: for if any were touched and awakened in publick, I should presently see him drop in to our private Meetings: [and] I was usually present with them, answering their Doubts, and silencing Objections, and moderating them in all.[5]

1. *R.B.*, I, ii, §41.
2. *Ibid.*, i, §§136 and 135.
3. *17*, preface.
4. *R.B.*, I, i, §135.
5. *Ibid.*, §137 (9).

It is not surprising that so thorough and sympathetic a pastor found ready response among his parishioners. Even so, only six hundred out of the eighteen hundred 'at age to be Communicants' responded so far as to accept the discipline which he proceeded to establish. 'Yet did I baptize all their Children; but made them first . . . give me privately, (or publickly if they had rather) an account of their Faith; [and] I rarely, if ever found both Father and Mother so destitute of knowledge and Faith, as in a Church Sense to be uncapable hereof.'

'With the Anabaptists to leave Infants unbaptized,' Baxter held, 'is injurious to Infants, and against the will of God'; though he could wish that, as in earlier days, 'no man was compelled to bring his Infants to Baptism, but all left to their own time'. He could not, however, hold infant baptism to be justified apart from the use of discipline: positively, in 'a Solemn Transition out of the state of Infant Church-Membership, into the state of Adult Church-Membership', 'due qualifications' being 'required', and 'the unfit' being 'left *inter Auditores,* without the Priviledges proper to Adult Members';[1] and negatively, in admonition and excommunication.

Both at this time and after his removal from Kidderminster Baxter was careful to insist that the practice of discipline was, and must be, entirely voluntary. Both 'the times' and 'our judgment' allowed 'us to use discipline upon none but such as consented to our office and relation to them': 'we could be Pastors to none against their wills'.[2] To the positive aspect of discipline few parishioners, perhaps, were likely to object. To 'give in their names, or any other way signifie' that they 'did own their Membership in this Parish Church, and take us for their Pastors', and for their pastors 'to keep their names, in a Church Book for memory, and to call them solemnly (at some day of humiliation, or other fit season) to own their Relation publikly', would not in itself offend them; nor could young converts take exception to making 'a Credible Profession of True Christianity', or a stranger to bringing 'a certificate (called of old Communicatory Letters)'.[3]

It was the negative aspect of discipline that men's pride, 'which is the most radicated and natural of all sins',[4] shied at. The method adopted at Kidderminster Baxter describes thus in a letter of 1656:

1. *Ibid.* (25).
2. *100,* pt ii, p. 185; cf. *R.B., loc. cit.*
3. *R.B.,* I, i, §§137 (25) and 171; *29,* p. 281.
4. *3* (3rd ed.), preface, fol. d4 verso.

As to my practice: I do, if it be secret, make the fault at first no more public than the owner made it, but secretly admonish him to repent and reform. If it be public, or if he repent not, and reform not, I admonish before two or three, and then call him to our meeting (where the representative church, *viz.* 2 presbyters, 4 deacons and 24 delegates meet once a month for such work) and there endeavour his humiliation and reformation. If he declare not repentance there, or if he do but return again to the sin, I do in the face of the congregation mention his crime, and our proceedings, and again with all seriousness and compassion there summon him to repentance: and if he refuse I desire the congregation to join in earnest prayer for him. This I do once or twice or thrice as prudence shall direct, considering the quality of the sin and sinner and the measure of the scandal. If yet he hear not the church, I do, from certain texts recited, require them to avoid him, and no more.[1]

'This was all we did, whether you call it Excommunication or not.' Excommunication was in fact exercised only on 'five or six young men that had got such a Love to tipling that they could not leave it'; for, apart from them, 'all the grosly ignorant, and the Common swearers, and all the Drunkards and scandalous persons were among the refusers' of discipline, while 'all sober, godly, well-minded Persons, if they once fell into any scandalous Action (as scarce two of them ever did), yea the very Civil and Younger sort that were tractable, did humbly confess their Sin, and walk more watchfully'.[2]

The lack of any attempt at such discipline was a long-standing ground for Puritan objection to contemporary episcopal or diocesan church order. 'Whilst the bishops ruled,' Baxter observes in his *Treatise of Episcopacy*, 'I never heard one man or woman called openly to repentance for any sin; nor one ever publikely confess or lament any sin. Nor one that was excommunicate in any Country where I came, except the Nonconformists.' Elsewhere he remarks that 'the private Work of Over-sight, and Ministerial Help' was 'a work that I never yet knew one Prelatist well perform, to my remembrance; and few of them meddle with it at all'.[3] In instituting at Kidderminster both the discipline and the pastoral oversight without which discipline could not be justified, he was a pioneer. Other ministers, first in Worcestershire and then more widely, showed an increasing readiness to attempt something similar. Yet

1. D.W.L. MS., 2:256.
2. *R.B.*, I, i, §137 (25); ii, §31; *100*, pt ii, p. 185.
3. *100*, pt ii, p. 184; *R.B.*, III, i, §8.

Baxter's was too much of a middle course not to excite disapproval from some for being too lax, from others for being too strict.

The model of discipline which he adopted had much in common, on the one hand, with that practised at this time in Congregational churches;[1] but he utterly condemned their schismatic way of gathering a congregation out of the parish, and held that the qualifications for church-membership which they demanded were too strict. 'To the Congregational Brethren I may boldly say, it is a Practice . . . suitable to your own Practice already; [but] be not Righteous over-much: Remember how tender Christ is of his little ones: and how he is displeased with those that keep them from him: and will not break the bruised Reed.' To the latitudinarians, on the other hand, who doubted the wisdom or benefit of 'such a Course of Discipline', Baxter admitted that 'those that were cast out of our Communion were enraged, and made much more Enemies to Godliness than before, though we exercised as much Patience and Tenderness towards them, as Reason could desire', adding, 'I never yet saw any signs of hope in any Excommunicate Person; . . . except one that humbled himself, and begged Absolution.' But he could not allow that this was the true criterion. 'We knew it to be an Ordinance of Christ, and greatly conducing to the Honour of the Church; which is not a common prophane Society, nor a Sty of Swine.' 'I would not have you be blind under pretence of Charity, nor to let in known swine, for feare of keeping out the sheep.'[2] 'An unsanctified Christian, and a Church not holy,' he asserted, 'are contradictions *in adjecto*'; and to the criticism, 'You are very severe in your Censure', he replied, 'I doubt some will find Christ more severe, and be less able to endure his Censure than mine.'[3]

Neither the pastoral oversight nor the discipline would have been possible for Baxter to attempt single-handed. In the former he was supported, as he always makes clear, by his assistants, especially Richard Sargeant (an ancestor of Joseph Chamberlain), who, 'when I put him to travel over the Parish . . . from House to House to Catechize and Instruct each Family', 'never grudged or seemed once unwilling', and 'I never heard of the Man or Woman

1. See G. F. Nuttall, *Visible Saints: the Congregational Way 1640–1660* (Oxford, 1957), pp. 127ff.
2. *29*, pp. 224ff.; *R.B.*, I, i, §137 (25).
3. *127*, p. 150f.

in all that Town and Parish . . . that once found fault with him'.[1]
At first Sargeant 'was always present while I did my work; and he
helped me in hearing them repeat the words, and then sat by while
I discoursed with them: by which means he quickly perceived the
way that I took'; and later 'the most bashful had rather go to him
than me, because they are bolder with him'.[2] Sargeant's successor,
Humphrey Waldron, 'was very much like him, and carried on his
work'.[3] Baxter was also assisted by Thomas Baldwin, 'our Schoolmaster at Kiderminster, sent to me by' Richard Vines, earlier a
companion of Baxter's at Coventry and now Master of Pembroke
College, Cambridge, 'an honest young Minister' who for a time had
'lived in my House, and learnt my proper Characters, or Short-
hand, in which I wrote my Sermon Notes'.[4] By 1656 all these
three men were in livings within easy reach of Kidderminster—
Sargeant at Stone, Waldron at Broom and Baldwin at Chaddesley
Corbett.

In 1657 Baxter's assistant was Joseph Read, a Kidderminster
boy whom, with another, Simon Potter, he had sent up to Trinity
College, Cambridge, with financial help from Lady Rous, Thomas
Foley and John Bridges. In 1653 the Master of Trinity, Thomas
Hill, wrote 'Potter and Read go on studiously, especially Potter,
they shall be pinched frequently'; and in 1656 his successor, John
Arrowsmith, wrote 'Your testimonial of Read came seasonably to
help forwarding the procuring of his degree. . . . Potter (now also
bachelor) is a very good youth, has been accordingly encouraged
. . . This day I have thought of a way which may perhaps take with
the Fellows, in order to his preferment'.[5] Potter's actual preferment was to the living of Wolverley, again near Kidderminster;
after a year with Baxter Read became Rector of Great Witley, where
Thomas Foley was patron. A third protégé of Baxter's at Cambridge, this time at Pembroke College, was Thomas Doelittle, later
Rector of St Alphage, London Wall, who 'whilst at school at
Kederminster heard' him preach the sermons 'afterwards printed
in his book of The Saints Rest', and between whom and 'his
spiritual father'[6] correspondence is still extant.

His successive assistants made Baxter's pastoral work easier,

1. *R.B.*, I, i, §137 (11).   2. D.W.L. MS., 3:188.
3. *R.B.*, loc. cit.   4. *R.B.*, III, i, §202 (22) and I, i, §173.
5. *R.B.*, I, i, §137 (13); D.W.L. MSS., 5:237 and 3:173.
6. [Jeremiah Smith,] memoir prefixed to Doelittle's posthumous
Complete Body of Practical Divinity (1723).

either by sharing in it or by relieving him of other duties. Discipline he could still not have established, he would perhaps hardly have envisaged it, without the support of his fellow-ministers in the county. From their first associating in 1653 they engaged themselves not only to the work of catechising but to mutual support in the exercise of discipline and 'agreed upon a Monthly Meeting at certain Market-Towns for Conference about Cases of Discipline as required Consultation and Consent: Accordingly at Evesham and Kiderminster they were constantly kept up'; and at Kidderminster, if offenders 'could not be prevailed with to repent' by Baxter and his assistant, 'we required them to meet all the Ministers at [this] other monthly Meeting, which was always the next Day after [the] parochial Meeting'.[1] Baxter had early shown his sense of the rightness of consultation between ministers when he sought the judgment of those at Coventry whether he should accept a chaplaincy in the army, and later whether he should continue in it. In establishing the Worcestershire Association he was again a pioneer. It was the first effective expression of his passionate desire for unity among men of differing judgments; and its acceptance in county after county as a pattern for collaboration contributed largely to the recognition of him as a national figure.

1. *R.B.*, I, ii, §31.

CHAPTER 4

The 'Meer Catholick'

BAXTER's desire for clarity in things of the mind, which led him constantly to categorise and subdivide, was accompanied, as we have seen, by an equally eager desire for unity in Christian faith and practice. Of the ten 'directions' to his people at Kidderminster, prefixed to *The Saints Everlasting Rest*, and summarised in the preceding chapter, by far the longest is the sixth, beginning, 'Above all, see that you be followers of Peace and Unitie, both in the Church and among your selves.' He continues:

He that is not a son of Peace is not a son of God. All other sins destroy the Church consequentially; but Division and Separation demolish it directly. . . . Many Doctrinal differences must be tolerated in a Church: And why? but for Unitie and Peace? Therefore Disunion and Separation is utterly intolerable. . . . Do not your hearts bleed to look upon the state of England? and to think how few Towns or Cities there be (where is any forwardness in Religion) that are not cut into shreds, and crumbled as to dust by Separations and Divisions?

It was always a source of gratitude and pride to Baxter that Worcestershire in general, and Kidderminster in particular, were without these separations and divisions. 'Our Unity and Concord was a great Advantage to us,' he wrote later, 'and our freedom from those Sects and Heresies which many other Places were infected with.' 'When People saw Diversity of Sects and Churches in any Place, it greatly hindered their Conversion; . . . But they had no such Offence or Objection' at Kidderminster, 'for we were all but as one'. In December 1659, towards the close of his ministry there, he could write, 'I know not of an Anabaptist, or Socinian, or Arminian, or Quaker, or Separatist, or any such sect in the Town where I live; except half a dozen Papists that never heard me.'[1] A year earlier he admitted, besides the Papists, the presence of 'one or two honest, ignorant Professours, that are turned Anabaptists, and joyne with the Church of them in the next Parish'.[2] This congregation, which had been gathered at Bewdley by the curate, John Tombes, itself numbered only 'about Twenty',

1. *39*, p. 43. 2. *29*, p. 165.

and the Baptists could claim 'perhaps as many more in the whole County'. 'At Worcester the Independents gathered' their church under Simon Moor, then Preacher at the Cathedral. Otherwise, 'I never knew of any of a divers Religion in all the County, save at the end, in one or two corners about Twenty Quakers: . . . and Two or Three ignorant Socinians.'[1] Elsewhere Baxter writes similarly of the Presbyterians, 'I knew but of one in all the County, Mr Tho. Hall',[2] Curate of King's Norton (then in the parish of Bromsgrove). For an experiment in Christian unity conditions in Worcestershire were thus favourable. To establish and foster such unity was the prime purpose of the Worcestershire Association which Baxter formed.

It was, indeed, fortunate for him that in Tombes of Bewdley he had an opponent worthy of him. Tombes was 'reputed the most Learned and able Anabaptist in England'.[3] Except for his insistence on believers' baptism, he had much in common with Baxter, like whom, when in 1662 he was ejected from the living of Leominster, Herefordshire, he adopted the position of a lay conformist. Despite a public dispute in 1650, which at the time occasioned a cloud of dust and for some years afterwards was continued in seemingly bitter published controversy, the two men remained good friends: to two tracts by Tombes written in 1660 against Quakers and Roman Catholics respectively Baxter wrote commendatory epistles. Baxter entered on the dispute, he said at the time, 'as Jonah to Nineve, against my will':

we have lived so long amongst contentions, and war, till our passions are become Gunpowder, and our memories Match, the one to catch fire, and other to keep it.

I can truly say, and without vanity [he added] that the chiefest study of my life is the Churches peace; and that all the controversal writings which I have written, or am about, are all to take men off from extreams, and bring them to Peace.[4]

In any case, despite the many books which he published in defence of infant baptism, Baxter did not regard its repudiation as an insurmountable barrier to unity, whether in spirit or in outward

---

1. *106*, ii, p. 186. The Quaker strongholds in Worcestershire were Evesham and Worcester.
2. *R.B.*, I, i, §140.
3. *Ibid.*, §137 (10).
4. *3* (3rd ed.), preface, fols. d4, e1 verso, e2 verso.

expression. To a correspondent anxious on her husband's and her own account about their duty with respect to baptism,

> There is a Connaturality of Spirit in the Saints [he wrote in 1658] that will work by Sympathy, and by closing uniting Inclinations, through greater Differences and Impediments than the external Act of Baptism: . . . I have an inward Sense in my Soul, that told me so feelingly in the reading of your Lines, that your Husband, and you, and I are one in our dear Lord, that if all the self-conceited Dividers in the World should contradict it on the account of Baptism, I could not believe them.[1]

Six years earlier he wrote thus to a correspondent engaged in a scheme for reconciling differences between parties: 'For Arminians & Anabaptists, they differ one in doctrinals, the other in part of worship: & I doubt not but they should be admitted, & we may easily accommodate for church union, or at least associative union, with all them that are peaceable.'[2] To this extent Baxter was on common ground with the practice of several Congregational churches, such as that gathered at Bedford in 1650, which, in the words of the title of a book by one who later became its minister, John Bunyan, saw in *Differences in Water Baptism No Bar to Communion*. In 1680 Baxter went so far as to say:

> In cases of necessity an open profession of Christianity, and entring into the Covenant of God, doth make a man a Christian even without baptism it self. . . . And it is a dishonourable doctrine against God and Christianity to say that God layeth his love and mans salvation so much on a Ceremony, as to damn or deny an upright holy soul for want of it. . . . The thing signified is necessary to salvation.[3]

To return to Worcestershire, and the Association of Ministers, the prime importance of which, alike to Baxter himself and to ministers throughout the country, is abundantly evident to a reader of his manuscript correspondence. It was not, it is worth observing, his success in Worcestershire which led him to entertain hopes of Christian unity more widely. On the contrary, it was his disappointment at the lack of response to his concern for unity on a national scale which drove him to do something in Worcestershire. 'We must try it, or only sit still and wish well as we had done.'[4] What was tried did not become public till the appearance in the summer of 1653 of *Christian Concord: or the Agreement of the*

1. *R.B.*, appendix iii, p. 54.   2. D.W.L. MS., 6:88.
3. *92*, 1st pag., p. 199.   4. *R.B.*, I, ii, §27.

Associated Pastors and Churches of Worcestershire; but the design was broached by Baxter at a meeting of ministers held in Worcester twelve months earlier. Although he then told them that 'the drawing up of a form for a profession of faith was a work for a whole Assembly of Divines', 'they imposed it upon me, to draw up a form of agreement'.[1] 'My greatest care,' he writes, 'was (especially in points not known by nature but only by supernatural revelation) to keep precisely to the very words of Scripture merely translated.' When some difference of opinion arose, whether or not the Deity of the Holy Spirit should be expressed explicitly, Baxter sought the advice of Archbishop Ussher—'I hope the reverend old man doth take it for the most honourable work of his age, to be instrumental for the Church's peace.' Ussher, though he 'thought it not fit to appear much for any new models', 'said that he would never refuse his best advice to any for peace and unity'; and in the event the exact formula concerning belief in 'God the Holy Ghost' which Ussher recommended, and which was written down in his presence, was adopted in *Christian Concord*.[2]

For 'the great name of that Reverend, Learned, Famous, Solid, Pious Divine, Bishop Usher'[3] Baxter had a regard perhaps greater than for any other of his contemporaries; but he was always eager to gain the advice and support of others, especially of scholars. As early as 1649 he was in correspondence 'about an attempt for Concord with all'[4] with the Masters of Pembroke and Trinity Colleges, Cambridge, and also with 'that man of admirable Learning, Humility, and Piety',[5] Thomas Gataker, the Rector of Rotherhithe, Surrey. His concern, however, he does not seem to have owed to any of his correspondents. It was his own, and what was laid on him was, he believed, of divine origin. 'God hath possessed my heart,' he wrote in 1653, 'with such a burning desire after the peace & unity of the churches that I cannot forget it, or lay it by.'[6] 'The Lord,' he wrote a year later, 'hath of late years . . . fastned in my soul so deep an Apprehension of the Evil of Dissentions, and of the Excellency and Necessity . . . of the healing of our Divisions, that it sticks in my thoughts night and day, and

---

1. D.W.L. MS., 5:236; *R.B.*, I, ii, §28.
2. D.W.L. MSS., 6:94 and 79.
3. *3* (3rd ed.), p. 335.
4. *R.B.*, I, ii, §26.
5. *57*, p. 596.
6. D.W.L. MS., 6:94.

the Zeal of such a Reconciliation doth eat me up.'[1] These are strong
words; but his achievement in and through the Worcestershire
Association answers to and justifies them.

Within the first three years of the Association's existence as
many as seventy-two ministers are known to have joined it.[2] Not
all of them were members at the same time: some died or left the
county, while others took their places. Nor were they all in
Worcestershire livings. Several were beneficed in Staffordshire,
three in Shropshire, two in Gloucestershire, one in Oxfordshire.
The Worcestershire members came from parishes in all seven
Worcestershire deaneries in the diocese of Worcester (as well as
from some of the Worcestershire parishes then in the diocese of
Hereford) and accounted for about a third of all the clergymen in
the county. Geographically, the county was covered fairly generally, from Old Swinford and the island of Dudley in the north to
Redmarley D'Abitot and the island of Blockley in the south, and
from Church Honeybourne and the island of Tredington in the
east to Shelsley Beauchamp and Clifton-upon-Teme in the west.[3]
The ministers who, with Baxter, were to the fore in forming the
Association and took a lead in its affairs were, naturally enough, in
livings in convenient proximity to Kidderminster. Three members
were, or became, moderate Independents, and one held, or
developed, Baptist convictions without actually renouncing infant
baptism. The others were not Presbyterians, save in the sense that
'the word *Puritane* is now vulgarly changed into *Presbyterian*'[4]: no
Presbyterian classis was formed in Worcestershire, and the
Association was composed solely of clergy. They included 'three
or four moderate conformists that were for the old Episcopacy;
and all the rest were meer Catholicks; Men of no Faction, nor
siding with any Party, but owning that which was good in all, as
far as they could discern it', 'neither Episcopal, Presbyterian nor
Independent, as to Parties; but desiring Union, and loving that
which is good in all'.[5] A considerable proportion of them probably
believed in fulfilling their ministry in whatever way changing

1. *8*, pt i, preface, fol. A3 verso.
2. See my analysis of the membership in *Journal of Ecclesiastical
History*, I, ii (October 1950), pp. 197–206.
3. Blockley is now in Gloucestershire, Tredington in Warwickshire.
4. *106*, ii, p. 84.
5. *R.B.*, I, i, §§140 and 137 (21); cf. I, ii, §23 ('the Vulgar called them
by the name of Presbyterians').

circumstances permitted. At the Restoration almost exactly half of the seventy-two whose names are known complied with the terms of the Act of Uniformity, and of those who did not and in consequence were ejected from their livings six conformed later.

'For a mixed organization of this kind' there was 'no previous precedent in England',[1] and the Association was significant even more in that it existed at all than in what it did; but it was far from idle. Of the monthly meetings planned to be held at Bromsgrove, Evesham, Kidderminster, Upton-on-Severn and Worcester, those at Evesham and Kidderminster 'were constantly kept up'. A general meeting was also held quarterly at Worcester. At Kidderminster, 'every first Thursday of the month was the Ministers meeting for Discipline and Disputation'. 'When we had dined together, we spent an Hour or two in Disputation on some Question which was chosen the Week before'; 'in those Disputations it fell to my lot to be almost constant Moderator: and for every such day (usually) I prepared a written Determination'. 'Many Ministers met with us, that were not of our Association, for the Benefit of these Disputations'; and 'I must confess', Baxter records, 'this was the comfortablest time of all my Life'. After the 'Disputation', difficult cases of discipline, and sometimes the offenders in person, were brought before the ministers,[2] as described in the last chapter. Besides attending this monthly meeting, some members of the Association also came to the lecture which Baxter delivered every Thursday; and afterwards 'I had the pleasant company of many of them at my House', 'with whom I spent that Afternoon in the truest Recreation, till my Neighbours came to meet for their Exercise of Repetition and Prayer'.[3]

Some of these 'Disputations', or his 'Determination' of them, are among Baxter's manuscripts at Dr Williams's Library. One, 'Whether the Infants of Notoriously ungodly baptized Parents have right to be Baptized', he printed in a volume which he dedicated to the Association, entitled *Certain Disputations* (1657), and three others in a further work, *The Safe Religion* (1657). Besides *Christian Concord*, the Association, or Baxter in its name, published in 1656 *The Agreement of divers ministers . . . in the county of Worcester . . .*

1. A. Gordon, *Heads of English Unitarian History* (1895), p. 65; Gordon points to one in Ireland.
2. For an agreement on behalf of the Association to admonish a drunken parishioner at Kidderminster, see D.W.L. MS., 4:131.
3. *R.B.*, I, ii, §§31 and 32 and i, §135.

for catechizing; and in 1658 *The Judgement and Advice of the assembly of the associated ministers of Worcestershire* concerning church unity. In 1660, 'though too late', as he ruefully records, Baxter also issued a small book entitled *Universal Concord*, 'that the World might see what our Religion and our Terms of Communion were; and that if after Ages prove more peaceable, they may have some light from those that went before them'.[1] The most notable of all the publications springing from the Association's labours was Baxter's *Gildas Salvianus; the Reformed Pastor* (1656), which Powicke justly calls 'the best written of all his books'.[2] Its occasion was the associated ministers' agreement to hold a special 'day of humiliation' at Worcester, in order to ask God's pardon for their neglect of their duty in catechising and His assistance as they now undertook it. Baxter, whom they had asked to preach at the meeting, was 'disabled from going thither . . . by the increase of my ordinary pain and weakness', and the ministers prevailed on him to publish what he had prepared. This book, which still repays perusal for its power to bring the reader close to a heart aflame, must always excite admiration for the Association which could endure, and even in part inspire, such prophetic preaching. Of late years it has been abridged by J. T. Wilkinson and anthologised by C. E. Surman.

The Association further interested itself in apologetic and in evangelism. Worcestershire proved less susceptible than did many counties to the inroads of Quakerism; but in 1654–5 Quaker preachers, itinerating two by two, left no county unvisited and Quaker tract-writers left few published pieces unanswered. Hostilities opened when in February 1655 two Quakers, Richard Farnworth and Thomas Goodaire, held a dispute at Chadwick, near Bromsgrove, with two leading members of the Association, Henry Oasland and Andrew Tristram, which Farnworth later recounted in print. As part of a calculated campaign throughout the country at this time the Quakers sent Oasland and also Baxter a paper of 'queries'. Both ministers replied, Baxter printing his retort as the second part of *The Quakers Catechism* (1655), which in turn was answered by the Quaker James Nayler. Goodaire meanwhile put into force the next stage in the campaign by the causing of a disturbance during divine worship. 'For asking Richard Baxter, in his place of worship in Kiderminster, How the

---

1. *Ibid.*, §197.   2. Powicke, i, p. 131, n. 2.

ministers of Christ & the ministers of Antichrist should bee knowne asunder', he 'was Imprisoned many weekes in the Castle prison in Worcester'. Farnworth then came to Worcester to Goodaire's aid, and in May both Quakers interrupted 'the great Rabbi', as Farnworth calls Baxter, 'att the time of a Lecter Sermon in Swithin Church, soe called, in Worcester',[1] with the consequence that Goodaire was returned to prison. The two bluff Yorkshiremen thus found themselves in the midst of a quarterly meeting of the Worcestershire Association. Farnworth proceeded to attack its *Agreement . . . for catechizing* in *A true Testimony against the Pope's ways*. To this Baxter made what he considered to be 'sufficient reply' in a paragraph in one of the prefaces to his *Reformed Pastor*.

The Association's brush with the Quakers no doubt heightened its awareness of the need for evangelising and securing against false doctrine 'every Place in the County that had need'.

Near one half of the Ministers . . . [as Baxter puts it] were a company of Poor weak Preachers, that . . . preached weakly that which is True, and lived in no gross notorious Sin. . . . Therefore we resolved that some of the abler Ministers should often voluntarily help them; but all the Care was how to do it without offending them.[2]

Now in November 1655 a number of Worcestershiremen in London, after a fashion already adopted by natives of Cheshire and Wiltshire and soon to be taken up by several other counties, had met for a sermon and a dinner. 'Being desirous to improve the opportunity for the good of our country', as the four of them appointed Stewards for the Worcestershire Feast wrote to Baxter, they had then collected '£37, which we hope to make up [to] £40 [as] a contribution towards the maintenance of a weekly lecture in our country for one year.'[3] This 'fell out seasonably' indeed. Baxter readily accepted the £30 sent him, and 'we covered all our Designs under the Name of the Londoners Lecture, which took off the Offence'. In an appendix to *The Reformed Pastor* he printed a letter signed by five other ministers and himself in the name of the Association, and addressed to 'all the rest of the ministers of the gospel in this county', explaining that Oasland and Tristram and two other ministers had been appointed 'every fourth Lords day to preach twice in those places where they shall judge their labours

1. *First Publishers of Truth*, edited by N. Penney (1907), pp. 277 and 275; Swarthmore MSS. (Friends House), 3:55 and 57.
2. *R.B.*, I, i, §137 (30).   3. D.W.L. MS., 4:83.

to be necessary: . . . we have no thought of obtruding their help upon you without your consent'; it 'proceedeth from the charity of our worthy countrymen in London'. For all his sharpness and outspokenness Baxter knew, in a phrase of Walter Cradock's, how to go 'the wisest way to work to win [men]'. 'This Lecture,' he wrote later, 'did a great deal of Good; and though the Londoners gave their Money but that one Year, yet, when it was once set on foot, we continued it voluntarily.'

The Stewards of the Worcestershire Feast chose Baxter as their correspondent and trustee. By this time he was generally recognised, to quote his Quaker opponent, as 'the chiefest Priest in Worcestershire'.[1] But it is hardly in doubt that they had heard also of the Association. They requested him to accept their money 'together with such others as you shall please to call to your assistance'. The Association had entered into correspondence with the Presbyterian Provincial Assembly in London as well as with one Association of ministers in Cumberland and Westmorland and with another in Ireland, and was becoming widely known.

To the letters sent in all these cases Baxter was the first signatory; and his private correspondence reveals the considerable part which he played personally in fostering the Association movement throughout the country. Cumberland and Westmorland, it is true, 'before we had heard of your book, had undertaken a work of the like nature'. The Cheshire Association, which was formed in October 1653, also seems to have come into being independently of Baxter; but this Association differed from that of Worcestershire, both in its narrower terms of admission and, from July 1655 onwards, in its inclusion of lay elders after the manner of a Presbyterian classis. 'Some of the ministers about Northampton,' Baxter heard in September 1653, 'are considering your *Agreement*, how it may be practicable among them.' The first county actually to form an Association on the Worcestershire model was Wiltshire. 'For your associating,' wrote Henry Bartlett, then Vicar of Fordingbridge, Hampshire, in October 1653, 'we are creeping after in these parts. Here at Sarum was yesterday a general meeting of all the well-affected ministers, a fast kept, then a solemn subscription to some general rules for associating, an agreement for a general meeting twice a year, the county divided into 4 parts, each to meet once in six weeks. We are beginning in Hampshire, and

1. R. Farnworth, *Antichrists Man of War* (1655), p. 17.

Dorset, but nothing yet done'. Four days later Peter Ince, Rector of Donhead St Mary, Wiltshire, sent Baxter what 'was subscribed by above 30 of us' on this occasion, with the comment 'I see we must drive gently or else we shall lose some honest company whom we would willingly have along with us'. In December Ince was able to report 'They be upon the like work in Dorsetshire & Somersetshire'; and by March 1654, 'The 12th of April is the general association in Dorsetshire. I have not seen the Kentish accord you write of.' In Kent a meeting was called for 17 April at Ashford but was deferred through the sudden death of the Curate of Maidstone, and 'we fear little will be done', wrote the Vicar of West Farleigh. In Somerset the dedications of ordination sermons provide evidence for the existence of an Association; and in December 1655 Baxter heard from Ince that 'They associated not long since in Devonshire.'[1] This association became one of the largest and most active in the country.[2]

By 1656 associations of ministers were also active in Cambridgeshire and in Cornwall. Both of these, like those in Cumberland and Westmorland and in Devon, took part in ordinations. This was a practice which neither the Worcestershire Association nor Baxter personally ever adopted, though both he and the Association desired an Act of Parliament to make such ordinations legal. In August 1656 the Rector of Buxted wrote that he had 'at last (though with much difficulty) prevailed with many godly ministers in our County of Sussex to subscribe to that work' of catechising, adding, 'Now I have dispersed many of your *Reformed Pastors* I hope few will stand out. We give your little book, *The Agreement*, to all the families in our parishes.' Two months earlier the Vicar of Shalford, Essex, lamented 'we here lie & do nothing. . . . I think there is no county in England where there is less work done as to conversion'. In time, however, Essex also had its Association. In April 1658 John Howe, then one of Oliver Cromwell's chaplains, wrote that its articles had been presented 'to his Highness (in order to the obtaining an approbation from him)'. The last Association to be formed was probably that in Norfolk, which published its *Agreement* in 1659. The movement had also continued to spread in counties nearer home. In August 1658 Baxter heard from the Vicar

---

1. D.W.L. MSS., 5:237, 3:163, 1:10, 1:8, 1:7, 5:60 and 5:72.
2. For the Devon Association, which was formed at Exeter on 18 October 1655, see Devonshire Association *Transactions* for 1877.

of Stretton Grandison, Herefordshire, 'We have long aimed at such
an association of the ministers of this county, as hath been happily
(& with much appearance of God's blessing) contrived amongst
you in Worcestershire. And our brethren have engaged me to
prepare the work by a public exhortation the first Tuesday of next
month'; and later in the month from the Rector of Uttoxeter,
Staffordshire, 'I hope the union and association of ministers (which
is now so much endeavoured after) may through God's blessing be
a great remedy against the present dangers of our Church. God
hath awakened the ministers of these parts to attempt such a work.'
To both these letters Baxter replied with gladness and serious
encouragement. 'The correspondency desirable between the
Churches at home and abroad . . .,' he wrote to the Herefordshire
minister, 'cannot be carried on with any but associated Churches.
The difficulties in your way in the people's unpreparedness are
more or less in every place.'[1]

These words may remind us that Baxter's concern for Christian
unity, though it found its most effectual expression in the parish
and the county, was not restricted to this sphere but was accompanied by an eagerness equally indefatigable for unity in the
nation and between nations. Anyone working for the desired end,
at whatever level and through whatever channels, whether purely
ecclesiastical or also political, was welcomed by him as a correspondent or in person. When in the course of theological controversy with him the Rector of Fawsley, Hampshire, referred to
'circumforaneous Legates . . . returning once in six or seven
moneths out of their circuits to their grand Master',[2] Baxter
indignantly repudiated the insinuation.[3] Nevertheless, his Hampshire, Dorset and Sussex correspondents do all gratefully recall
visits to Kidderminster; Baxter also thanks Howe for visiting him;
and in his letter to the Rector of Uttoxeter he writes of 'Mr Dury'
as 'even now with me'. This was the Scottish free-lance theologian
John Dury, who at the time was Librarian at St James's. Until this
century Dury has been lost in the oblivion which is the usual lot
of the ineffectual; but high tribute is now accorded him as a pioneer
ecumenist, and deservedly. He 'presents a remarkable example of
a life which was wholly devoted to the service of reconciliation and

---

1. D.W.L. MSS., 5:105; 3:106, 198 and 135; 1:247; 3:139.
2. John Crandon, *Mr Baxter's Aphorisms Exorized* (1654), epistle
dedicatory.
3. *8*, pt v, p. 12f.

unity': 'no apostle of Protestant unity was more indefatigable or resourceful'.[1] That he and Baxter should find themselves drawn together was thus almost inevitable.

Of the years (1652-8) during which he was in touch with Baxter, Dury spent three (1654-7) abroad in the endeavour, with letters of commendation from the Protector and both the universities, to foster Christian unity in Switzerland, Germany and the Netherlands. His visit to Baxter in August 1658 followed a letter enclosing a 'packet of papers', 'of each paper one copy for yourself, & the other for the Association', whereby 'you will see how far the foreign Reformed Churches are engaged . . . with the countenance of their magistrates to maintain a Correspondency . . . one with another & with us'.[2] To the Worcestershire Association Dury wrote: 'You have been the first that have given an example unto others of associating; & therefore must not be the last in my thoughts, to gain your assent & concurrent advice how to proceed.'[3] Between 1652 and 1654, when apart from a visit to Stockholm Dury had been in London, Baxter and he were in regular correspondence over a scheme to encourage unity in this country by the holding of a conference. This plan originated not with Dury but with Baxter, who two months before his first letter to Dury had written to the Master of Trinity College, Cambridge, urging the university's support for 'a petition to the Parliament, that they would set up a few of the 4 parties (Presb: Indep. Episcop. Erast.) together (men of greatest ability & moderation & interest) to find a temperament wherein all may agree'.[4] To Dury Baxter went so far as to suggest suitable names from each of the parties mentioned. Two years later, in April 1654, after 'unwearied solicitations' to attain the purpose desired, Dury was able to report 'several considerable meetings' between 'the chief leading men of the Independent & Presbyterian brethren'. 'At last five of each side have been deputed, to whom the future proceedings and preparatives of a full agreement are referred.' These ten representatives duly met '& set

1. M. Schmidt and N. Sykes in *History of the Ecumenical Movement*, edited by R. Rouse and S. C. Neill (1954), pp. 97 and 134.

2. D.W.L. MS., 1:74.

3. *Ibid.*, 76, with the titles of thirteen papers, one not hitherto attributed to Dury. The MSS. also include the Association's reply to Dury, both a longer version in Latin and the English version which Dury printed. Dury was also in correspondence with the Devon Association at this time.

4. *Ibid.*, 3:272.

themselves in a course to proceed which I hope will produce some blessed effect'.[1]

At this point the driving force was removed by Dury's going abroad; and the conference, which in any case represented but two of the four parties which Baxter desired to bring together, had, it would seem, no effect at all. At the same time, seven of the ministers 'deputed' by their brethren had in fact just been appointed by Cromwell to serve among the Commissioners for the Approbation of Preachers (commonly called the Triers); while at least two of them had been present at meetings called earlier on his own account by Cromwell, who had 'made a proposal much to the same effect' as Baxter's in 1652 and who had continued, Dury informed Baxter, 'forward in the work'.[2] In 1658 Baxter still felt able to assure John Howe that 'the Lord Protector is noted as a man of catholic spirit, desirous of the unity & peace of all the servants of Christ'.[3]

After the Restoration Baxter's integrity forced him reluctantly to acknowledge that under Cromwell 'Godliness had Countenance and Reputation also, as well as Liberty', and to 'bless God who gave me even under an Usurper whom I opposed, such Liberty and Advantage to preach his Gospel with Success, which I cannot have under a King to whom I have sworn and performed true Subjection and Obedience'.[4] Nevertheless, Cromwell was a usurper; and this precluded easy co-operation with him or his government. Together with four other members of the Association Baxter did go so far as to accept office as a Worcestershire Assistant to the Triers; yet only half-heartedly. 'I refused to try any under them upon their reference,' he writes, 'except a very few, whose Importunity and necessity moved me (they being such as for their Episcopal Judgment, or some such Cause, the Triers were like to have rejected)'.[5] Parliament's authority remained, however, and he was aware how desirable, indeed necessary, it was to have Parliament's support in his efforts after unity on a national scale, if these

1. *Ibid.*, 6:82. For fuller quotation from Baxter's correspondence with Dury, see my article in Presbyterian Historical Society *Journal*, X, i (May 1952), pp. 4–15. The correspondence appears not to have been used in the studies of Dury which have been published in this century in London, Chicago, Marburg and Uppsala.
2. *Ibid.*, 6:83; 5:199.
3. *Ibid.*, 3:200.
4. *R.B.*, I, i, §137 (4).
5. *Ibid.*, §116.

were to be at all effectual. For the *Humble Petition* about which he had written to the Master of Trinity, he did not gain the approval he desired from the University, but it was signed by many thousands of Worcestershiremen, including the mayors of Evesham and Worcester. On 22 December 1652 it was duly presented to Parliament by two of his most loyal friends in the county, John Bridges and Thomas Foley; and 'the House gave a kind and promising Answer to it'. Besides asking that 'some of the most godly, prudent, peaceable Divines of each party' might be called together to discover 'a meet way for accommodation and unity', the petition urged provision for both the university education and the financial maintenance of the ministry. This last demand inevitably drew Quaker fire. 'I wrote a Defence of it,' Baxter records, 'and caused one of them to be given each Parliament Man at the Door'; but 'within one day after they were dissolved'.[1]

With the Parliament which sat from July to December 1653, the 'Little' Parliament whose members were nominated by the Independent churches in each county, Baxter was naturally not in sympathy: it was but 'another Pageant to be played'. But in 1654 there was again something more nearly approaching a representative Parliament, and accordingly he renewed his endeavours. In August he had occasion to preach at the Worcester Assizes before John Glynne, then Justice of Assize for the Oxford circuit (in which Worcester falls), and newly elected member for Caernarvonshire in the Parliament about to assemble. In an epistle prefixed to this sermon which, as the first part of *True Christianity* (1655), was published at the judge's request, Baxter urged Glynne and all other members of Parliament 'to promote one Scripture-Creed, or Confession of Faith, agreed on by a general assembly of able Ministers, duely and freely chosen hereunto', together with 'a publique establishment of the necessary liberty of the Churches'.

This time, no doubt to Baxter's surprise, what he desired came about. A conference was called. The decision was taken so soon after Parliament met that it can hardly have been in response to his plea in *True Christianity*, though copies of the book (dated 1655) were in circulation in London and Hampshire in the first week of November 1654. He must have been still more surprised to find himself among the ministers summoned to London, there to assist a sub-committee appointed to confer with the Protector about the

1. *Ibid.*, §112.

articles of religion in the Instrument of Government which provided the protectorate with its constitutional basis. He was informed of the summons in a letter written on the day of his appointment (4 November) by one of the members for Dorset, Thomas Grove, of Berry Court, Donhead St Mary, Wiltshire, the parish of which Baxter's friend Ince was Rector. Grove had presented Ince, and with Ince had been to visit Baxter in 1652. 'Come and help us,' he now wrote; 'I am glad to hear that you have every week the opportunity of a coach'; and, after naming the other ministers summoned, 'You may wonder at the miscellany but it was thought fit to have men of several interests and judgements.'[1]

The list of names in Grove's letter is identical neither with the list in the manuscript of Baxter's autobiography of those whom he found already in conference when he arrived, nor with that in another manuscript in his own hand;[2] but among the names are those of five of the ministers who had met seven months earlier in the conference organised by Dury, while two of them were among those originally suggested by Baxter himself. Some of those nominated evidently declined to serve, among them Archbishop Ussher; and though Grove did not say so it was as a substitute for Ussher that Baxter was nominated. He could hardly have had a greater compliment, at least in his own eyes, all the more if (as he indicates in one manuscript account) it was Ussher himself who had suggested his name to the M.P. who had nominated Ussher. This was Roger Boyle, Lord Broghill, member for Cork and also one of Cromwell's Council of State. Despite 'great Weakness and Soporous or Scotomatical Ilness of my Head', Baxter lost no time in making for London. 'The brethren of our Association,' the Vicar of Blockley wrote to him on New Year's Day 1655, '(though they never sent to you) have been mindful of you at the throne of grace. . . . We doubt not but you will prosecute the motions made in your epistle to Serjeant Glynne before your Assize-Sermons.'[3]

Baxter's experience of the conference was a sorry one. 'The over-Orthodox Doctors', he complains, insisted on inserting among the 'Fundamentals of Religion' many 'crude and unsound Passages' not in Scripture. In March 1652, in his letter to the Master of

---

1. D.W.L. MS., 3:169.
2. *Ibid.*, 9:113, printed (with omission of one name deleted in MS.) in *R.B.*, I, ii, §50; and D.W.L. MS., 8:92, printed in *Monthly Repository*, xx (1825), pp. 287ff.
3. *Ibid.*, 3:174.

Trinity, he had written with reference to some *Humble Proposals* which a group of Independents was then making to Parliament, 'I hear the Independents are now about cutting out all themselves.' The men who took the lead at the present conference were all four of them Independents from this earlier group, and *The Principles of Faith* (1654) which, despite Baxter's caustic and cogent criticisms, were agreed on, approved by Parliament and printed, were no more than a fresh issue of their earlier *Proposals*. Baxter thus had good grounds for his comment that 'the tincture of Faction stuck so upon their Minds, that it hindered their Judgment'. In any case, with the dissolution of Parliament in January 1655, once more 'all came to nothing, and that Labour was lost'.[1]

Bitterly disappointing as this visit to London was, it brought Baxter a measure of prominence and public recognition which he never attained again. For some of the time he was Grove's guest, but in the main 'I lodged at the Lord Broghill's'.[2] The country parson found his fame as a preacher had preceded him and now brought great crowds to hear his sermons. At St Laurence Jewry, where one of these, published as *Making light of Christ and Salvation* (1655), was preached, the Vicar, his friend Richard Vines, 'was fain to get up into the Pulpit, and sit behind me, and I to stand between his Legs'; and Broghill and his brother-in-law, the Earl of Suffolk, who had brought Baxter by coach, 'were fain to go home again, because they could not come within hearing', leaving it to the Earl of Warwick, 'who stood in the Alley',[3] to bring him home again. On 17 December, before the Lord Mayor and 'to the greatest Auditory that I ever saw',[4] he preached at St Paul's Cathedral *A Sermon of Judgment* (1655). A week later, on Christmas Eve, he preached twice: at St Martin's and in Westminster Abbey. The former sermon, 'shewing the great necessity of Unity in real Holiness', he published 'with enlargement' as *Catholick Unity* (1660);[5] part of the latter, 'a few Directions which I then gave the Parliament Men for Church Reformation', 'was taken by some one' else and printed as *Humble Advice* (1655). On yet another occasion,

1. *R.B.*, I, ii, §§55, 53 and 56.
2. *Ibid.*, §60.
3. *Ibid.*, i, §165, accepting A. G. Matthews's emendation of *Abbey* to *Alley* (i.e. Aisle).
4. *Ibid.*, §166.
5. *Ibid.*, §167; the date at the end of this sermon (1657) is a misprint.

by the good offices of Broghill and Warwick, he preached before the Protector 'on I. Cor. 1.10, against the Divisions and Distractions of the Church'.[1] This was not well received and was not printed. It led to Cromwell's sending for him, and the two men twice spent four or five hours together; but with no result save that the earlier estrangement between them was deepened. In the presence of Lambert and Thurloe as well as Broghill, Baxter 'dealt so plainly with' Cromwell 'as cast him into . . . Passion'.[2] 'I saw,' Baxter says, 'that what he learned must be from himself.'[3] It is a shrewd comment but Cromwell might have said it of Baxter with equal truth.

Far more memorable than these visits to the Protector were Baxter's meetings with 'the most Reverend, Learned, Humble, and Pious Primate of Ireland, Archbishop Usher, then living at the Earl of Peterborough's House in Martin's-Lane. Sometimes he came to me, and oft I went to him.' When Baxter told Ussher of his objections to the behaviour of the Independents at the conference, Ussher shared them. He also asserted 'the validity of Presbyters Ordination' and 'owned' as his the important paper later published as A Reduction of Episcopacie (1656). For long Baxter had reverenced no one more deeply than Ussher, and the number of his references in later years to these meetings with the archbishop show how great a privilege and undergirding he held them to be. When in the following summer he offered the deprived Bishop of Exeter terms for communion with episcopal divines, he told him Ussher had said that 'with moderate Men they might suffice for an Union'.[4] Two years later we find him writing to an Independent, 'I am left only reconciled to a certain sort of episcopacy (such as Bishop Usher and I did agree in, in half an hour)'.[5] That Ussher returned Baxter's regard is clear from the fact that a few weeks before his death he gave instructions for a copy to be sent to Baxter of his latest book, De Graeca Septuaginta (1655). It is not surprising that to Lord Broghill, to whom was owing not only the summons to London in the first place, with all the crowded experiences of those few weeks, but above all his new acquaintance with Ussher, Baxter dedicated his own next book, The Unreasonableness of Infidelity (1655).

1. Ibid., §164 and ii, §57.   2. 103, pt iii, p. 102.
3. R.B., I, ii, §59.   4. Ibid., §37; cf. §§46 and 62.
5. D.W.L. MS., 3:115; cf. R.B., I, ii, §76.

During the next five years Baxter had no further occasion to present his convictions in London with the added force of his presence; but he still lost no opportunity of pressing them by his writings. When in the summer of 1656 elections for a new parliament took place, he received a letter from Edward Harley, now re-elected member for Herefordshire. Harley requested him 'to assist me with your direction how to move in this ensuing Parliament for the service of the distressed Church. For I am sure that only *Fata Ecclesiae* can auspiciate *Fata Imperii*. I pray God take away the scandal of schism, no less dangerous than the scandal of the cross.' Baxter's many pages in reply, marked by his unfailing clarity, with enumerated divisions and subdivisions, can now be read in full in Professor Schlatter's study, *Richard Baxter and Puritan Politics*.[1] With a glance back at 'some leading men' whom he had found 'exceeding forward . . . to swerve from Scripture phrase', he laid it down that 'forms imposed to be subscribed should be from Scripture to a word' and assured Harley 'I could tell you in a few words' what Ussher 'and I agreed in half an hour'. 'Let some further means be tried,' he asked once more, 'for the reconciling of the Presbyterians, Independents and Prelatical. A free chosen convocation is best in its season.' He also showed a continuing concern for the maintenance of the ministry and for education.

We saw in the previous chapter something of his efforts to secure for some of his younger parishioners the university education which he had missed himself. In September 1657 Matthew Poole, then Rector of St Michael-le-Querne, London, wrote for Baxter's judgement on a plan to establish a trust for maintaining poor students at the universities. Baxter thought the scheme 'an excellent good one'—'But I pray you lay not your design so low as 8 score *li*. per annum; I should hope that the London ministers agreeing on it might promote it to many 100 *li*. per annum'[2]—; and when Poole's *Model for the Maintaining of Students* appeared in April 1658, it duly included a commendatory epistle by Baxter. A passage from this will show the practical, passionate nature of his concern, which was far from being narrowly academic.

Papists are up, and Atheists and Infidels and Jewes are up, and abundance of secret Apostates are up openly reproaching the Ministry, that privately deride Christ and the Scripture, and the Life to come,

1. New Brunswick, N.J. (1957).   2. D.W.L. MS., 6:217.

(I know what I say to be true). Quakers are up, and all the prophane as farre as they dare: And shall not we be up to further that Gospel and Ministry and Church of Christ, which so many bands of the Prince of darknesse are armed to assault. . . .

It would make a mans heart ake to think of the dark state of the world, for want of Preachers. Were it but the state of Ireland and Wales, it should move us to compassion.

The reference to Wales points to yet another of Baxter's interests. Concern for the state of Wales was common among the Puritans at this time, when more than sixty free schools were set up within the Principality. Few besides Baxter saw the need not only for schools but for university education and even a University of Wales. In his first letter of support for Poole's scheme he suggested that Poole should 'let the natives (now in London) of every county know . . . And thus you might help Wales also, for many would give in compassion to Wales, that else will not do it.' Next year, at the end of a 'Preface to the Nobility' in a book entitled *The Crucifying of the World* he printed a 'Catalogue of seasonable Good Works'; and here, immediately following the maintenance at the universities of students for the ministry, 'to erect a Colledge (at Salop, I think the only fit place, for many Reasons) for the education of Scholars for the use of Wales' finds its place as 'a blessed Work for our Rulers and some Rich men'. In this matter he was in regular correspondence with a Commissioner for the Propagation of the Gospel in Wales and J.P. for Cardiganshire, John Lewis, of Glasgrug, Llanbadarn Fawr. Lewis, as Baxter puts it, 'joined with me in a design to have begg'd Money in Pity to Wales, to have set up a Welsh Colledge at Shrewsbury'.[1]

The catholic compassion which drew out Baxter's heart 'in Pity to Wales' drew it overseas as well. 'No part of my Prayers,' he wrote, 'are so deeply serious, as that for the Conversion of the Infidel and Ungodly World';[2] and the tenth and last of the 'seasonable good works' which he commended was 'to erect a college' for the training of ministers to undertake 'the conversion of some of the vast nations of infidels'. By going among them 'with the plain and pure gospel', Baxter believed men were 'like to do

---

1. *135*, p. 128f. For this correspondence, see my article in Merioneth Historical and Record Society *Journal*, II, ii (November 1954), pp. 120–34; and for Baxter's continuing concern for Wales in the changed circumstances after the Restoration, see *The Beginnings of Nonconformity* (Hibbert Lectures, 1962), by G. F. Nuttall and others (1964), ch. i.

2. *R.B.*, I, i, §213 (23).

much more good' than the Jesuits, 'as Mr Elliot and his helpers find of their blessed labours in New England'. John Eliot, who spent almost sixty years in indefatigable labours to convert the Indians, for whom single-handed he translated the Bible into their language, has a high place among pioneers in the history of Protestant missionary enterprise. His correspondence with Baxter opened in 1656, when he wrote to thank him for *The Saints Everlasting Rest*. Baxter replied 'that anything of mine should be useful to you is matter of thankfulness to God; but it is as *his*, and not as mine'. 'I know no work in all the world,' he continued, 'that I think more highly and honourably of than yours; and consequently no person whom I more honour for his work sake.'[1] The two men continued to correspond for many years. As late as 1682, at the end of a book fittingly entitled *Obedient Patience*, Baxter still referred with admiration to what 'old Mr John Eliots, and his helpers' had done 'by long unwearied labour'.[2]

'Dear Sir,' he wrote in his first letter to Eliot, 'were it not an excellent work for the pastors of your church to join in an earnest persuasive to union to the Presbyterian and Congregational brethren in England . . .?' Eliot's principles were Congregational, and many of his letters are concerned with ecclesiology. Poole, on the other hand, was a *jure divino* Presbyterian, who valued Baxter's collaboration partly because Baxter had 'so great an interest among all, particularly among many of the Episcopal way'.[3] The Welshman John Lewis was a conservative who not only objected to the Puritan prohibition of the observance of Christmas Day but argued for 'the use & necessity of solemnities (for rites & ceremonies I dare not call them for the odium against the very names) for the setting forth the reverence of divine worship'. Baxter's correspondence, no less than his actions, show the genuineness of his claim to catholicity. With none of these three men did he see eye to eye at every point; but with each of them he was eager to work in the interest of the things which united them. He would have warmed to these words of a 'mechanick' unordained Baptist preacher: 'I do not love any man the more or less for his judgments sake, whether he be Presbyterian, Independent, Baptized, &c. But

1. For Baxter's correspondence with Eliot, see John Rylands Library *Bulletin*, xv, 2 (July 1931).
2. p. 269.
3. D.W.L. MS., 3:39.

wherever I see the Image of Christ appear (which is love and holiness) there I desire to love and honour'.[1]

Baxter's own 'confident and setled Judgment' was that each party 'had some Truths in peculiar . . . and each one had their proper Mistakes'.[2] 'You could not (except a Catholick Christian) have trulier called me,' he wrote towards the end of his life, 'than an Episcopal-Presbyterian-Independent.'[3] 'Dear brother,' he wrote once to his Wiltshire friend, Peter Ince:

bottom upon Christ and the great fundamentals. Unite in those with men of holiness & righteousness. Prosecute that union affectionately & unweariedly: & keep your eye upon that glory where we shall be one.[4]

1. Thomas Ewins, *The Church of Christ in Bristol* (1657), 68 (misprinted 60).
2. *R.B.*, I, ii, §1.
3. *103*, pt i, p. 110.
4. D.W.L. MS., 1:11.

CHAPTER 5

The Mere Nonconformist

On 1 May 1660 Parliament voted to recall Charles II; and on 29 May the King entered London amid great rejoicing. In the events immediately preceding his restoration Baxter took a significant part. For the last two and a half years he had been in regular correspondence with a man whom it is difficult to picture in the gallery of his friends: the Earl (later Duke) of Lauderdale, whose character was a blend of 'sensuality, cruelty and hypocrisy'[1] but who had occupied himself, while a political prisoner in Windsor Castle, with translating for Baxter's use passages from a French book against popery. In March, following General Monk's entry into London, Lauderdale was released and sent word to Baxter that he desired to see him on matters of state. Baxter accordingly travelled to London, where he arrived on 13 April. He was immediately visited by Lauderdale, who was already in touch with the King, with 'expressions of extraordinary kindness'.[2] What this means appears from an account written many years later in which Baxter says that the King 'sent D[uke] Lauderdale to me purposely to invite me to receive the Testification of his Favour and Acceptance'.[3] He was also visited by Sir William Morice, who in February had with the King's approval become Secretary of State, and by James Sharpe (later Archbishop of St Andrews), who at this time, like Morice, was an agent of Monk.

During the previous year, when 'few Men saw any probability' of the King's return, Baxter had published a book entitled *The Holy Commonwealth*. He had also dedicated two books to Richard Cromwell as Lord Protector. He was now won to the royalist cause; and for a time he found himself back in the prominence he had enjoyed on his visit to London five years earlier. The day before Parliament voted the King's recall he preached *A Sermon*

1. Powicke's summary, ii, p. 44.
2. D.W.L. MSS., 9:118 verso, from a passage not printed in *R.B.* but printed by Powicke, i, 189, and also in Lloyd Thomas's abridgment of Baxter's autobiography.
3. *134*, p. 43.

of Repentance (1660) at St Margaret's, Westminster; and on 10 May he followed this with a sermon preached before the Lord Mayor at St Paul's Cathedral, which he published as *Right Rejoycing* (1660). In the first sermon he mentioned once again that Ussher and he had agreed on church government 'in less than half an hours debate';[1] and as a consequence 'many moderate Episcopal Divines came to me to know what those Terms of our Agreement were'.[2] In the second sermon he thanked God that the restoration of the monarchy was being effected 'with little or no effusion at all of blood'.[3]

He was not among the ministers in the party which went to the Netherlands to accompany the King back to England. Nor, from the terms in which he describes Charles's entry into London, was he among 'the London Ministers in their Places' who then acclaimed the King. He was not, after all, a London minister. But on 25 June, with other 'Chief Presbyterians', he became a Chaplain to the King; and on the same day, through the good offices of his friend Lord Broghill, who had urged him to accept the chaplaincy, he took a leading part in an audience granted the new chaplains. The King 'gave us . . . as gracious an Answer as we could expect' and professed his determination to reach agreement in ecclesiastical matters 'by abating somewhat on both sides, and meeting in the Midway'.[4] A month later, on 22 July, Baxter preached before the King and published his sermon as *The Life of Faith* (1660) by royal command.

So far so good. The prospect might seem set fair for realising the kind of 'accommodation' which Baxter had long sought, and for his returning to Kidderminster justifiably satisfied with his own share in having brought it about. The future was in fact entirely otherwise. There would be no accommodation, nor even any permanent return to Kidderminster. These last three months of hopefulness and sudden prominence were to be followed by two years of increasing frustration, and they by nearly thirty more of inactivity and disgrace. He never preached again before the King. He did preach a series of sermons in Westminster Abbey 'before many members of the honourable House of Commons'; but when these were published, the epistle to the reader contained the following sentences.

1. *43*, p. 42. 2. *R.B.*, I, ii, §80.
3. *44*, p. 48. 4. *R.B.*, I, ii, §§82 and 88–91.

A low, despised, suffering state, is that believers must ordinarily expect, and prepare for, and study to be serviceable in. If better (may I call it better) come, take it as a feast, and grudge not when the table is withdrawn; and look not it should be our every days fare.

The title of these sermons was *The Vain Religion of the Formal Hypocrite*. The date of the passage quoted was 15 November 1660. What had happened since July?

One sign of the change in the barometer was the passing on 13 September of the Act for Confirming and Restoring of Ministers. This provided for the return to their livings of clergy sequestered since 1643. It was an inevitable step in any genuine restoration and not more than three hundred clergy were immediately affected by it. Baxter, however, was one of them; for at Kidderminster 'the old Reading Vicar', George Dance, was still living and now recovered his benefice. This may explain why a sermon by Baxter, which ten days later Samuel Pepys went to the Abbey in hopes of hearing, Pepys calls Baxter's 'farewell sermon'. A little earlier, Baxter had been chagrined by the behaviour of Thomas Pierce, who 'went up and down raging' with a denial that Baxter's *Life of Faith* had been published by royal command, even that Baxter held the office of Chaplain to the King at all. This was nonsense, but it was a straw in the wind; for Pierce was 'a Man, whom the Diocesan Party . . . much gloried in'. Meanwhile, at the King's request, Baxter with other ministers drew up a 'Paper of Proposals', with Ussher's *Reduction of Episcopacie* appended, 'as a Ground-work towards an Accommodation'; but from 'the Episcopal Divines there came nothing to us, but a Paper of bitter Opposition'. It next became clear that the King's intended 'Declaration . . . concerning Ecclesiastical Affairs', a draft of which the ministers received on 4 September prior to its publication, 'would not serve to heal our Differences'. They drew up a petition to the King, again pleading for 'Primitive Episcopacy' as distinct from diocesan, but 'were never called to present it'. Finally, a conference between the two parties, held in the King's presence at Worcester House on 22 October, proved utterly fruitless. Baxter left it 'dejected'.[1]

It was at this juncture that he received overtures concerning the see of Hereford. The first hint that he was to be offered it reached him shortly before the conference at Worcester House; three days

1. *R.B.*, III, i, §150; I, ii, §§116, 96, 101, 106f. and 114.

after the meeting, on the day of the publication of the King's *Declaration*, the Lord Chancellor himself, Edward Hyde, asked him if he would accept a bishopric. He took a week to decide. 'My Judgment was fully resolved against the Lawfulness of the old Diocesan form'[1] of episcopacy. In the royal *Declaration* as now published were unexpected alterations representing concessions on this point, but he doubted (rightly, as it proved) whether the *Declaration* would ever have the force of law. Three days later again, on 28 October, the first new bishops were consecrated in Westminster Abbey, all to dioceses: among them Gilbert Sheldon to the see of London and George Morley to that of Worcester. On 1 November Baxter sent the Lord Chancellor a courteous refusal, 'specially because it will very much disable me from an effectual promoting of the Church's Peace'.[2] It was a remarkable reason to offer for declining to be a bishop but events were soon to justify it. 'By the close of 1660,' a student of the Restoration judges, 'it must have seemed likely to all observers that the Church would be re-established in the old form';[3] and in that re-establishment it was the insistence on episcopacy in the old form which within two years had rent the Church irreparably. Baxter ventured to suggest the names of seventeen men, all country clergy like himself, whom he thought suitable for such preferment. None of them was chosen. The new Bishop of Hereford, who was appointed on 1 December, was General Monk's brother Nicholas, who four months earlier had been created Doctor of Divinity at Oxford at the King's command on account of his 'particular and eminent sufferings and service for our self and the Church, during the late distractions'.[4] Baxter, not finding himself free to become a bishop in the Church, was soon to be deprived of all legal share in its ministry. The table was withdrawn.

During the following year Baxter was a member of a Royal Commission 'to advise upon and review' the Book of Common Prayer 'and if occasion be, to make such reasonable and necessary Alterations, Corrections and Amendments therein, as . . . shall be agreed upon'. The Commission was set up on 25 March 1661 and

1. *Ibid.*, §121, where the word 'Frame' printed by Sylvester is a misreading of the MS. 'forme'.
2. *Ibid.*, §123.
3. Anne Whiteman, in *From Uniformity to Unity 1662–1962*, edited by G. F. Nuttall and O. Chadwick, p. 75.
4. Anthony Wood, *Athenae Oxonienses* (1691–2), ii, p. 812.

was allowed four months in which to complete its report. To Baxter's part in this Savoy Conference, as from its venue it has come to be known, more attention has been paid than to any other equally brief period in his life. It was indeed an important conference, and he knew it to be so. His elucidation of the course it took, documented by numerous *pièces justicatifs* and finished with vivid characterisations of the participants, covers more than sixty pages of his autobiography. His own contribution to the conference, as the leader on his side, was second to none; and the 'Reformed Liturgy'[1] which he drew up for it was a remarkable achievement, even without regard to the fact that he composed it within a fortnight.

The Savoy Conference proved as fruitless as the earlier meeting at Worcester House. The Commissioners reported that they were 'agreed on the Ends, for the Churches Welfare' but 'disagreed of the means'.[2] For this dismal outcome it is usual to blame Baxter: to say that at the Savoy he appears at his weakest, blundering in his strategy and utterly lacking in *finesse*.

This, though undeniable, is not wholly fair. From near the beginning of the proceedings, or even before, Baxter recognised that hope of agreement was doomed. 'I foreknew and foretold them what they were about to do': 'I perceived that they intended no Abatements.'[3] In these circumstances, clear statement was called for rather than bringing into play what little diplomacy he possessed. When his friends, who were no more hopeful than he, were for abandoning the debate, Baxter demurred. 'It's better let the case be seen in writing,' he argued, 'than so break off.'[4]

It is also fair to remember that it is his own papers which provide the material for adverse judgement on his management of affairs. In a sense, he would have welcomed this result of their publication; 'I have a strong love to Truth,' he wrote, '. . . and specially a love to historical Truth';[5] and 'that History is credible', he laid it down elsewhere, 'which consentingly speaketh against the known interest of the Author'.[6] He assembled these papers, which later in the year 'somebody printed', not for the sake of his own reputation but

1. Printed in *48*.
2. *R.B.*, I, ii, §231.
3. *Ibid.*, §212.
4. *106*, ii, p. 240.
5. *116*, pt ii, postscript, fol. M3.
6. *91*, 'What History is Credible, and what not', fol. a1 verso.

because he was determined that 'every word', 'exact and all', should be 'on Record to the Notice of Posterity'.[1]

The question remains whether he was justified in his attitude to the conference, or whether by his pessimism he made agreement impossible. Put bluntly, 'could the conference have succeeded, had Baxter not been a member of it?'[2] This question is asked in the most recent full investigation of what passed at the Savoy; and the answer the writer gives is negative. While the conference was in session, on 8 May, the new Parliament met; and later that month the few members who would not receive the sacrament according to the order of the Prayer Book were suspended. Before the conference had ended, in the fortnight between 25 June and 9 July, a Bill for Uniformity, assuming conformity to the Prayer Book as it then stood, was read three times in the House of Commons. Baxter could not be unaware of these developments. Nor could it escape him that, with the restoration of the bishops to the House of Lords, all twelve principal commissioners on the episcopal side now had seats in that House, to which on 10 July the Bill for Uniformity was sent up: that (literally, if not in the sense the phrase normally carries) they were playing a double game. In the following January some of them, in fact, served on the Lords' Select Committee for the Bill.

During the latter half of 1661 Baxter turned from national concerns to the endeavour to secure some foothold for his ministry in Kidderminster or at least in the diocese of Worcester. He was unsuccessful at both levels, as unsuccessful as at the Savoy. A petition for his return to Kidderminster from 1,600 communicants was of no avail. Dance, whom Baxter had treated with consideration in respect of his vicarage as well as of his legal claim to a fifth of his stipend, now that his thirteen years of sequestration were over was not willing to allow Baxter to return on any terms whatever. He not only disregarded his bond of twenty years earlier to admit Baxter as Lecturer but refused Baxter's offer either to act as his curate or to serve as preacher in an honorary capacity. He would not even allow him to hold a farewell service of preaching and sacrament with his former flock. Baxter's rooms in Kidderminster were his own, and he once again enjoyed 'a Meeting of many Ministers' there. Privately, he even preached there and once

1. *R.B.*, I, i, §208; ii, §§261, 233 and 113.
2. E. C. Ratcliff, in *From Uniformity to Unity 1662–1962*, p. 127.

or twice in other houses; but Dance then 'denied me liberty to preach any more' at all and 'a certain Knight'—presumably Sir Ralph Clare, for it was he who 'was the principal Cause of my Removal'—'offered the Bishop his Troop to apprehend me, if I offered to preach'.[1]

Baxter then went to see the bishop of the diocese. It was unfortunate for him that the new bishop was George Morley: for at the Savoy Conference he had found Morley to be 'the chief Speaker of all the Bishops, and the greatest Interrupter of us', while 'it was my lot to contradict him'. Morley utterly refused to license Baxter to preach in his diocese, and thereafter Baxter never did so. After a final leavetaking from his people at Kidderminster, 'I need not say, with mutual sense and tears',[2] he never returned to the place where 'I once thought my days would have been ended'.[3] On 11 November he inserted a brief account of what had happened in a book then coming out of the press, but even this led to controversy in print with the bishop. In January seventeen of his former parishioners, including some of the feoffees who had invited him to Kidderminster twenty years earlier, wrote sorrowfully lamenting 'this violent rending of you from us'. This letter must have meant much to Baxter; but he 'for many years forbore so much as to write any letters'[4] to his Kidderminster friends, 'lest it should bring Suffering upon them'.[5]

In London he still had some liberty. During the Savoy Conference Sheldon as Bishop of London had exercised his right to prevent Baxter's election by the London clergy as their Proctor in Convocation from coming into force. Earlier in the year, however, Sheldon had granted him a licence, which is still among his manuscripts,[6] to preach in the diocese of London; and with this authorisation Baxter preached regularly on both Sundays and weekdays during 1661 and the first half of 1662 in a number of city churches, and published some of his sermons as *The Mischiefs of Self-Ignorance* (1662).

Of his other activities during 1662 little is known: partly for a reason to be mentioned shortly, but mainly, one surmises, because

1. *R.B.*, I, ii, §§256, 247, 152 and 249.
2. *Ibid.*, §§236, 268 and 253.
3. *50*, epistle to inhabitants of Kidderminster.
4. D.W.L. MSS., 5:142 and 4:232.
5. *R.B.*, I, ii, §254.
6. See *Baxter Treatises*, edited by R. Thomas, p. 10b.

the shades of the prison-house were closing in, increasingly limiting what he could do and also making the memory of it afterwards too bitter to record. It is not surprising that he became 'somewhat wearied' and even 'was oft thinking to go beyond Sea, that I might find some place in retired privacy to live and end my days in quietness'. On 20 December 1661 an Act was passed requiring all members of Corporations to abjure the Solemn League and Covenant of 1643, and twelve months before election to receive the Lord's Supper according to the rites of the Church of England; whereupon all but one of the Burgesses at Kidderminster 'were turned out'.[1] The months dragged on. Under various clauses of the Act for Confirming and Restoring of Ministers some hundreds more clergy were ejected. The Bill for Uniformity became steadily more rigid and exacting as it went to and fro between Lords and Commons. The end cannot have been in doubt, only its date. On 19 May 1662 the Act received the royal assent and the date for the ejection of clergy not episcopally ordained and unable to give unfeigned consent and assent to everything in the Prayer Book was set at 24 August. This was the ninetieth anniversary of the Massacre of St Bartholomew in France. It was also just a month before the ministers would normally receive their tithes.

Baxter possessed episcopal ordination and was not opposed to the Prayer Book in principle. But to a Church established on terms intended to exclude he could not conform. The 'meer Catholick' could not be other than a Nonconformist. He did not wait till 24 August. After a farewell sermon from Colossians 2:6–7 at St Anne's, Blackfriars, he ceased preaching at once. In a famous phrase, 'I would let all Ministers in England understand in time, whether I intended to Conform or not.' In all probability his example had considerable influence; but this can have brought him little comfort. The things for which he cared and had laboured without rest had crumbled before him. The Voluntary Associations of ministers throughout the country were as if they had never been. All in all, 'about one thousand eight hundred or Two thousand Ministers were Silenced and Cast out'; and now 'a great Inundation of Calamities . . . overwhelmed Thousands of godly Christians'.[2] Kidderminster was left, as his friends there had written,

1. *R.B.*, I, ii, §§274 and 254.
2. *Ibid.*, §§278–80. The figure is remarkably near that computed for England only by A. G. Matthews in *Calamy Revised* (Oxford, 1937), which is 1760.

'scattered as sheep upon the mountains, without our shepherd'.[1]
For himself, his grief and vexation must have been intolerable.

> And that one Talent which is death to hide
> Lodg'd with me useless!

Patience to prevent that murmur came no more easily to Baxter
than to Milton. 'For these six years time,' he could write six years
later, 'in which I thought my greater experience, had made me
more capable, of serving my Master better than before, his Wisdom
and Justice, have caused me to spend in grievous silence.'[2] At the
time, all he knew was that he was cast into 'Groans and Tears
which I can never on Earth forget'.[3]

The darkness which thus descended on him, and which was
never completely to lift during his life, was broken by one brilliant
shaft of light. Little more than a fortnight after St Bartholomew's
day, on 10 September 1662, he was married to a woman of strong
character and courage who entered intelligently into his convictions
and shared with eager affection whatever suffering or deprivation
they were to bring him. The remembered image of Baxter is
mainly, and justly, of the Vicar of Kidderminster, who was
unmarried; and to the end he preserved objectivity of judgement
of a kind suggesting the detachment of a naturally celibate mind.
Even after his marriage he not only recorded his belief that for
himself at Kidderminster 'my single Life afforded me much
advantage' but commended celibacy for ministers in general; and
among the 'conditions of our marriage' he laid it down 'that she
would expect none of my time which my Ministerial work should
require'. In the event his wife proved 'the meetest helper that I
could have had in the world'. 'The danger of Imprisonment, and
paying £40 for every Sermon' never led her 'to hinder or dis-
courage me from any one Sermon'; and it is touching to observe
how in the memoir of her written after her death Baxter attributes
to his wife's decision and initiative actions which in the autobiography composed while she was still alive he describes as his
own.[4]

Margaret Charlton was a Shropshire woman, 'of one of the chief
Families in the County', the Charltons of Apley Castle, near

1. D.W.L. MSS., 5:142.
2. 58, epistle to church at Kidderminster.
3. 116, pt ii, postscript, fol. N2 verso.
4. R.B., I, i, §137 (16); 71, 1st pag., p. 482f.; 97, pp. 47, 70 and 61.

Wellington, where she was born in 1636. She was thus twenty-one years younger than Baxter and at the time of their wedding not much more than half his age, an 'unsuitableness' which, he admits, 'made our marriage the matter of much publick talk and wonder'.[1] She had come with her mother to Kidderminster in 1656, and after a period in Oxford at Christ Church, where her brother-in-law, Ambrose Upton, was then a Canon, had returned to her mother permanently. From the extracts from her intimate papers which after her death Baxter saw fit to publish, it is not easy to disentangle exactly what happened; but so much is clear. Towards the end of his ministry in Kidderminster, a serious illness and recovery from it led to the young woman's conversion; she believed she owed her life as well as her soul to his prayers; and when in April 1660 he left Kidderminster for London, she found that she could not bear to be parted from him, and with her mother followed him to London. They took lodgings in Sweetings Alley, off Threadneedle Street, close to Austin Friars, where Baxter was then living with his old friend, Thomas Foley; and here in the following January her mother died.

On the extent of their association in London before they were married Baxter is naturally reticent. At the time, equally naturally, others were not so. 'It was famed at the Court that I was married . . . near a year before it came to pass';[2] and by 31 March 1662 a letter, addressed to Baxter at his physician, Dr John Micklethwaite's house in Little Britain, off Aldersgate, to which he had now removed, could convey a greeting 'may I not say to your espoused wife'.[3] On 29 April 'Richard Baxter of St Buttolphs Aldersgate' (Micklethwaite's parish) and 'Margaret Charleton of Christ Church' Newgate (the parish adjacent) were granted a licence to be married at Christ Church.[4] Their marriage on 10 September took place, however, not at Christ Church but at St Bennet-finck, close by, and was performed by the newly ejected Curate of that church, another old friend of Baxter's, Samuel Clark.

For Baxter to be persuaded to marry this young and well-to-do woman—'her Portion . . . was £2,000'—was a remarkable turn of

1. 97, pp. 1 and 46.
2. R.B., I, ii, §275.
3. D.W.L. MSS., 4:191.
4. Cambridge University Library MSS., 7450.d.21: see photograph facing p. 43 of J. T. Wilkinson's edition (1928) of Baxter's Breviate.

events; and any observation of their life together confirms one's inclination to suppose that it was she who did the persuading. 'She was apt when she set her mind and heart upon some good work . . .,' her husband wrote of her, 'to be too much pleased in her expectations and self made promises of the success': who then more suited to be the partner of one who describes himself as 'naturally of a discouraged spirit'? If the Vicar of Kidderminster was clearly a bachelor, it is no less clear that the ejected minister would scarcely have survived without his wife. 'I had never known much worldly cares,' he admits ingenuously; 'before I was Married, I had no need: afterwards she took the care on her.' 'In very hard cases, about what was to be done,' he adds, 'she would suddenly open all the way that was to be opened'; and 'my experience usually told me, that she was in the right, and knew more than I.'[1]

Henceforth, as he puts it in the memoir of her which he published after her death, 'we lived in inviolated love, and mutual complacency, sensible of the benefit of mutual help'. They had their difficulties, of course: a woman of some education, as is apparent from the handwriting and manner of her letters, she 'thought I had done better to have written fewer Books, and to have done those few better'; but 'these near nineteen years I know not that ever we had any breach in point of love'. Her understanding of personal problems was such that 'of late years', Baxter says, 'I confess, that I was used to put all, save secret cases, to her, and hear what she could say'; and her underlying faith such that 'for near these Nineteen years that I have lived with her, I think I never heard her thrice speak a doubting word of her Salvation, but oft of her hopeful perswasions, that we should live together in Heaven'.[2] That she became his wife at this precise point in his life, when his work was in ruins and there was no hope of its recovery, revealed, as another ejected minister justly claimed at the time of her death, 'the real greatness of her Spirit'.[3] From his side Baxter frankly states that his exclusion from pastoral charge made him more willing to enter the married state: 'some of my disswading Reasons were then over'.[4]

1. 97, pp. 47f., 76 and 66f.; *R.B.*, I, i, §136.
2. 97, pp. 47, 73 and 68f.
3. John Howe, *Funeral Sermon on the Decease of . . . Margaret Baxter* (1681), p. 40.
4. 97, p. 47.

For most of the first year after his marriage Baxter remained in London, in a house in Moorfields. On the ground of 'having incurred already so much hatred and displeasure by endeavouring Unity', he 'medled but little' with what further sporadic and ineffectual endeavours there were to procure the 'comprehension' (then the term in use) of Nonconformists within the Church of England or, at the least, an 'indulgence' to them in line with the King's promises at Breda. He went so far as to visit the Lord Chancellor with a view to gaining Hyde's 'preconsent' that 'the Citizens of each County' might provide some maintenance for the ejected 'Ministers of that County' without risk of being charged with conspiracy; but he would not join in petitioning for an enlargement of their liberty. 'As we were forbidden to preach, so we were vigilantly watcht in private, that we might not exhort one another or pray together.' Baxter refrained from public preaching, but he could not bring himself to decline every invitation to a 'Meeting for Prayer'. On one such occasion he was nearly arrested. It became known that he and some other ministers were to meet to pray with a dying woman, and two justices were sent 'with the Parliaments Serjeant at Arms, to Apprehend us'. In the event Baxter was prevented from attending the meeting. 'They came upon them into the Room where the Gentlewoman lay ready to die, and drew the Curtains, and took some of their Names, but missing of their Prey, returned disappointed.'[1]

During this twelvemonth two leading London ministers, for both of whom, despite their opposite temperaments, Baxter had a peculiar respect as men 'of the Primitive Simplicity', 'of the Primitive Sincerity', died: Simeon Ashe, the Rector of St Austin's, 'one of our oldest Non-conformists', and James Nalton, the ejected Rector of St Leonard's, Foster Lane. Ashe was buried 'the very Even of Bartholomew-day', Nalton on the first day of 1663, and Baxter was with each of them towards the end, with Ashe indeed on 'his last Evening'. If, as it seems he did, he felt their deaths as signalising the passing of an age, his feeling was confirmed in the following June by the death of William Juxon, 'the old peaceable Archbishop of Canterbury'. Juxon's successor, Gilbert Sheldon, had licensed Baxter to preach in the diocese of London; but Baxter was not unaware that 'all Men supposed'[2] Sheldon, with

1. *R.B.*, I, ii, §§278, 418, 427, 426, 283 and 422.
2. *Ibid.*, §§420f., 425 and 236.

the Bishop of Worcester, to have taken a leading part (none the less effectual for his absence from most of its sittings) in directing the Savoy Conference. With Sheldon now officially, as well as in fact, at the head of affairs, it was clear that the cloud of suspicion and forced inactivity would not be lifted.

'Sheldon,' Dr Bosher has written, 'was the product of a world which, if not dead, was fast dying.'[1] This is true. Baxter's lot was to live through its death-pangs. Nonconformists could look for nothing but perpetual exclusion. On 30 June 1663, 'instead of Indulgence and Comprehension', the Conventicle Act, forbidding meetings for religious purposes other than according to the Prayer Book, with more than four persons present beyond the members of a single family, 'past the House of Commons, and shortly after was made a Law'. Baxter accordingly decided to leave London, which in any case he says he found deleterious to both health and study. 'All Publick Service being at an end, I betook my self to live in the Country (at Acton) that I might set my self to writing, and do what Service I could for Posterity, and live as much as possibly I could out of the World. Thither I came 1663. July 14.'[2]

For the next six years he continued in a retirement only rarely disturbed and gave himself more than ever to his writing. In 1664 he published a devotional book entitled *The Divine Life* and three years later a more considerable work of apologetics, *Reasons for the Christian Religion*. *A Cure of Church Divisions*, which appeared in 1670, was also written at Acton. So was his enormous folio *A Christian Directory*, though he could not get this licensed for publication till 1673. He did succeed in seeing through the press a few anonymous tracts of an evangelistic and edifying nature. He also wrote commendatory prefaces for books by three other ejected ministers and had a weighty letter, on the proportion of one's income which one should give to charity, included in a fourth's. He naturally kept up his extensive correspondence: mostly with other Nonconformist ministers, but also with ministers on the Continent and in New England, where Eliot and Eliot's missionary labours were as dear to him as ever. It was in fact largely owing to Baxter, the Company's 'staunchest ally',[3] as its historian describes him, that the New England Company was continued in being after

1. R. S. Bosher, *The Making of the Restoration Settlement* (1951), p. 265.
2. *R.B.*, I, ii, §§428 and 439.
3. W. Kellaway, *The New England Company 1649–1776* (1961), p. 41.

the Restoration, with Robert Boyle as its new Governor; four letters from Baxter are preserved among Boyle's manuscripts in the Library of the Royal Society in London.[1]

Apart from 'spending now and then a day in London', Baxter remained in Acton for practically the whole of this period. The one exception was when, during the Great Plague of 1665, he removed to 'the House of my dearly beloved and honoured Friend Mr Richard Hampden of Hampden in Buckinghamshire', where he used the occasion to work on his autobiography: the end of its second part is dated 'Hampden, Septemb.28.1665'. His reference to the Plague is characteristic in being at once vivid and precise.

The Plague which began at Acton, July 29.1665 being ceased on March 1. following, I returned home; and found the Church-yard like a plow'd field with Graves, and many of my Neighbours dead; but my House (near the Church-yard) uninfected, and that part of my Family, which I left there, all safe, thro' the great mercy of God, my merciful Protector.[2]

Of the Great Fire which followed in September he laments especially 'the Loss of Books' as 'an exceeding great Detriment to the Interest of Piety and Learning' and records: 'I saw the half burnt Leaves of Books near my Dwelling at Acton six miles from London'.[3]

The thing which Baxter valued most at Acton was the acquaintance, indeed the friendship, which he formed during his last year there with Sir Matthew Hale, then Lord Chief Baron of the Exchequer and shortly to become Lord Chief Justice, 'a Neighbour whom I cannot easily praise above his worth'. 'I lived then in a small house,' Baxter relates, 'but it had a pleasant garden and backside' which were attractive to Hale. Hale 'bought it, and lived in that poor house', which 'was indeed well scituate, but very small', while Baxter moved into 'a great House of great Rent'. Both houses are now gone; but the former was photographed before it was pulled down in 1898 and the site of each is known. The 'great House' was 'over-against the Church-door', which proved indeed a circumstance most unfortunate.

In his acquaintance with Sir Matthew Hale, Baxter found in this

1. See *Notes and Records of the Royal Society*, xiii, 2 (November 1958), pp. 141, 149, 171 and 181.
2. *R.B.*, I, ii, §§439 and 445; III, i, §28.
3. *Ibid.*, III, i, §31.

time of inactivity and frustration the same sort of special satisfaction which, when at the height of his influence, his briefer
meetings with Ussher had brought him. It is indeed a picture
pleasant to dwell on, the great divine and the great judge—'the
pillar of Justice, the Refuge of the subject who feared Oppression,
and one of the greatest Honours of his Majestie's Government'—
meeting, and talking, and listening to each other. Baxter, who
admits his own 'too much forwardness to speak', lays great stress
on the listening, which perhaps he learned from Hale, who 'was a
Man of no quick utterance, but often hesitant; but spake with
great reason'.[1] What did they talk of, besides the great lawyer,
John Selden (to whom Hale was an executor) and Selden's
antipathy to Hobbes? Gilbert Burnet, who after Hale's death in
1676 published his *Life* (1682), writes: 'their Conversation lay
most in Metaphysical and abstracted Idea's and Schemes'.[2] Baxter
bears this out. In the *Additional Notes* (1682) to Burnet's *Life*
which he issued, he says: 'almost all our discourse was Philosophi-
cal, and especially about the Nature of Spirits and superior
Regions; and the Nature, Operations and Immortality of mans
Soul'.[3] Tradition in Acton points to the sculptured heads either
side the west doorway of the parish church as preserving the
association of the two men; and that their likeness was intended
seems undeniable.

We have a vignette of Baxter during these years at Acton from
the pen of an admiring visitor. In his diary for 1667 Henry
Newcome, now ejected from his preachership at the Collegiate
Church (today the Cathedral) in Manchester, has the following
entry:

On May 10th, Mr Ashurst went with me to Acton, to see Mr Baxter.
He put me upon family duty; and I found myself very dry and unfit,
being tossed about, and very highway-like. He preached to his own
family after dinner on I Thess.iv.17,18. He was discoursing before, that
he had great comfort against the great sin of unwillingness to die, from
the consideration of a glorified mediator, and in his sermon he discoursed
rarely of it.[4]

This preaching in his own house was what brought Baxter into
trouble and eventually drove him from Acton. The tenth of May

1. *Ibid.*, §§106f., 129; *110*, epistle to reader and pp. 4, 9 and 24.
2. p. 75.   3. *110*, p. 4f.
4. *Autobiography of Henry Newcome (ut sup.)*, ii, p. 165. 'Highway-like'
means ordinary, mediocre.

1667 was a Friday; but he was also accustomed to preach on a Sunday after attending Common-Prayer at the parish church, and not his own family only: 'a few poor Neighbours . . . came in'. It was not a wise thing to do. Two years earlier, 'as I was preaching in a Private House, where we received the Lord's Supper, a Bullet came in at the Window among us, and past by me, and narrowly mist the Head of a Sister-in-law of mine that was there'. He persisted, and after the expiration of the Conventicle Act 'there came so many that I wanted room', until 'almost all the Town and Parish, besides abundance from Brainford [Brentford], and the Neighbour-Parishes came'. This no doubt had its part in his removal to a larger house; but it could not commend him to the non-resident rector, Bruno Ryves, the Dean of Windsor, who was also Dean of Wolverhampton, where he lived, or to Ryves's curate, 'a weak, dull young Man, that spent most of his time in Ale-houses, and read a few dry Sentences to the People but once a day'[1]—Kidderminster in 1641 all over again!

Sir Matthew Hale did not attend these meetings; but he told Baxter 'he thought that my course did the Church much service'; and 'when the People crowded in and out of my House to hear, he openly shewed me so great respect before them at the Door, and never spake a word against it, as was no small encouragement to the Common People to go on'. In Wolverhampton the minister ejected from the living, John Reynolds, was one day so exasperated that he indiscreetly referred to Ryves's permitting conventicles at Acton. This set up a train of events which led, on 12 June 1669, to Baxter's arrest under the Act of 1665 prohibiting ejected ministers from coming within five miles of an incorporated town, and to his imprisonment in Clerkenwell. His release after no more than a week or two was technically on an error in the warrant; but the 'Character' of Baxter which Hale gave 'openly, at the Table of Serjeant's Inn, before the rest of the Judges' had much to do with it. Hale's distress at his arrest had burst out into tears—'the only time', Baxter says, 'that ever I saw him weep'.[2]

Baxter's reflections on his imprisonment are revealing.

My Imprisonment was at present no great Suffering to me, for I had an honest Jaylor, who shewed me all the Kindness he could; I had a large room, and the liberty of walking in a fair Garden; and my Wife

1. *R.B.*, I, ii, §440f.; III, i, §§102 and 104.
2. *110*, p. 24f.; *R.B.*, III, i, §§107, 128 and 126.

was never so chearful a Companion to me as in Prison, and was very much against my seeking to be released, and she had brought so many Necessaries, that we kept House as contentedly and comfortably as at home.[1]

He felt it keenly that he was deprived of public worship. He also found the summer heat oppressive, and complained of the 'noise of Prisoners just under me every Night' and 'the number of Visiters by day' as the one interfering with his sleep, the other with his studies. Even so, the preface to the second part of his book *Directions for Weak Distempered Christians* (1669) is dated 'From my lodging in New-Prison, June 14.1669'. To his visitors he would say that

the loss of one Grain of Love, was worse than a long Imprisonment: And that it much more concerned us, to be sure that we deserved not Suffering, than that we be delivered from it: [and]
If Passion made me lose my Love, or my Religion, the Loss would be my own. And Truth did not change, because I was in a Goal [jail].[2]

He returned to Acton for 'but a few hours hastily, to let my house', for now 'I must go out of Middlesex'. He went not far away to the neighbouring county of Hertfordshire, to 'a few mean Rooms . . . extreamly smoaky and . . . cold', 'part of a poor Farmers', at Totteridge, near Barnet. Here he spent the winter, still writing, 'in a troublesome, poor, smoaky, suffocating Room, in the midst of daily pains of the Sciatica, and many worse'. Yet 'when violence separated me from my too much beloved Library, and drove me into a poor and smoaky House, I never had more help of God, nor did more difficult work than there!'[3]

Some years later Baxter's brother-in-law, Francis Charlton, was living at Totteridge, and it has been suggested that this may have drawn Baxter to go there; but Charlton's relationship to the Baxters was unfriendly, nor is it certain that he had yet come to Totteridge. The village may have commended itself as a chapelry attached to the distant parish of Hatfield in the diocese of the far-away Lincoln, and thus likely to provide freedom from ecclesiastical interference. More probably the attraction was the presence there of 'my most faithful and familiar friend', John Corbet, the ejected

1. *R.B.*, III, i, §119; cf. 97, p. 51: 'she brought her best bed thither'.
2. *R.B.*, III, i, §§119 and 125.
3. D.W.L. MSS., 6:108; *R.B.*, III, i, §§129, 132 and 147; 97, p. 51; *114*, p. 227.

Rector of Bramshott, Hampshire, whom Baxter had first met at
Gloucester in 1642. For when on 23 June 1670 Baxter and his wife
removed to another house in Totteridge, 'which we took to our
selves', it was large enough to accommodate not only themselves
and Baxter's stepmother but Corbet and his wife. Corbet's 'great
love drew him . . . to remove' to be with Baxter, who found great
benefit from the company of this 'Man of extraordinary Judgment,
stayedness, moderation, peaceable Principles, and blameless life';
'in all the time that he was with me, I remember not . . . that ever
we had one displeasing word'. The two men's wives also became
fast friends. When in 1673 the Baxters returned to London, the
Corbets had already left Totteridge for Chichester; but after
Corbet's death in December 1680 his widow came back to be
companion to Baxter's wife and was at her bedside when she died
six months later.[1]

The reason for the two men's going their own ways again was
simply that opportunity offered for the resumption of their
ministry. For in March 1672 Charles II issued a Declaration of
Indulgence to Nonconformists, permitting both meeting-places for
worship and 'teachers' to be licensed. Ten years' exclusion and
persecution had done no more than suppress Dissent: licences
were taken out in all the fifty-two counties of England and Wales
save Anglesey. Corbet's 'old flock at Chichester', where in 1648 he
had been Preacher at the Cathedral, invited him back and on 1 May
he was duly licensed there as a Presbyterian 'teacher'. Baxter was
far more hesitant. In the first place, he distrusted the King's
motive: the Nonconformists knew, he says, that 'the Toleration
was not chiefly for their sakes, but for the Papists'. He also saw
that what was connived at by royal indulgence was still illegal and
that the permission granted could easily be withdrawn—as within
a year it was. At a deeper level, to him 'indulgence' or such
'toleration' was unwelcome because it undid all his hopes of
'comprehension' or 'accommodation' within the Church of
England. The Declaration required the use of denominational
distinctions in the licences granted; and this not only, as he says,
'tended to continue our divisions' within Nonconformity, it would
also have the effect of welding Dissent as a whole into a hard lump,
proudly conscious of the differences between itself and the Church
which Baxter was eager to see dissolved. In 1672 to perceive this

1. *R.B.*, III, i, §§171 and 206 and ii, §66; *97*, p. 52; *105*, p. 27.

was so shrewd that it appeared fractious; but a generation later it
is what actually happened. The Toleration Act of 1689 did in fact
draw hard and fast the main lines of Nonconformity as a permanent
element in the English scene; and the word 'denomination',
from meaning no more than a party name, has come to signify
an organised institution with its own traditions and vested
interests.[1]

For some months, therefore, Baxter forbore to apply for a
licence; but on 25 October he wrote to a friend at court as follows:
'I hear that Licenses have been denied some who will not take them
in the name of some sect, Independent, Presbyterian, or Anabaptist or such like, or as Preachers to such a sect, which I cannot
do'. 'If you please to procure me one as a mere Nonconformist,' he
continued, 'I shall thankfully accept it.' To this request he sub-
joined a statement of what he called 'my Case'. In this he says,
'My Religion is meerly Christian; but as rejecting the Papal
Monarchy and its attendant evils, I am a Protestant.'[2] Two days
later the requisite licence was granted, and granted not only, as he
desired, under the general head of 'a Nonconforming Minister' but
'to teach in any licensed or allowed Place'.[3] He still waited a few
weeks. 'The 19th of November (my Baptism-Day),' he records,
'was the first Day after ten Years Silence, that I preached in a
tolerated Publick Assembly (though not yet tolerated in any
Consecrated Church) but only (against Law) in my own House.'[4]
One can hardly miss the sadness and frustration in this halting
sentence.

In appearance there was probably little difference between what
Baxter did now and what he had been doing at Acton and latterly
also at Totteridge, where he says of his wife that 'out of Church-
time, she gladly opened her doors to her Neighbours that would
come in for instruction'. In fact, however, it was the beginning of
a new period in his life. His wife could no longer be content with
his confinement at Totteridge. 'She was earnest with me to go
[to London] for the exercise of my ministry.' First he delivered
four lectures at Pinner's Hall on a foundation (which still exists)
then newly set up for the protection of the principles of the
Reformation; but these, to his chagrin, gave offence theologically.

1. *105*, p. 28; *R.B.*, III, i, §214.
2. cf. *Baxter Treatises*, edited by R. Thomas, p. 15a.
3. *Original Records*, edited by G. L. Turner (1911), i, p. 575.
4. *R.B.*, III, i, §226.

In January 1673 he began to preach on Fridays, in an honorary capacity, at a meeting-house in Fetter Lane built in 1666. In February his wife followed this up by taking a 'most pleasant and convenient house in Southampton-Square' (now Bloomsbury Square), where his physician, Thomas Cox, also lived; and 'after Easter' he 'removed thither with my Family'.[1] By this time the Declaration of Indulgence was already rescinded; but, having begun, Baxter continued to preach as opportunity offered and made London his home till his death in 1691.

The story of the next eight years is a strange tangle, with the unchanging basic pattern of schemes by Baxter's wife to enable him to preach and schemes by others to prevent him. We are not left in doubt how much he owed to his wife's practical initiative and financial generosity. 'She saw me too dull and backward to seek any Employment till I was called,' he admits; so 'she first fisht out of me in what place I most desired more Preaching'. His reply was, 'St Martin's Parish, where are said to be forty thousand more than can come into the Church, especially among all the new Buildings at St Jameses, where Neighbours many live like Americans.' They were among 'the most ignorant, Atheistical, and Popish about London', he understood. His wife proceeded to take 'divers Rooms over the Market-house' at St James's on a short lease and 'to importune me to preach each morning', though it was 'an inconvenient place' and also (despite being a new building) proved dangerous from inadequate support for its heavy roof. For the conduct of the service, 'the Greatest part' of which was ordered according to the Prayer-Book, 'though none of the Common Prayers were used', Baxter's former assistant at Kidderminster, Joseph Read, who in 1661 had been ejected from his Worcestershire living, was brought up to London, probably also by Mrs Baxter's means; for, when Read took a house near Baxter's in Dyott Street (off Great Russell Street), 'my Wife urged the building of another Meeting-Place' there, and Baxter preached there as well. He was not left untroubled for long. Before the lease of the market-house at St James's had expired he was prosecuted, ineffectively, under the Second Act against Conventicles of 1670; and in the spring of 1675 he was prosecuted again over his lecture —now on a Thursday—at Fetter Lane, but again without effect. 'I that had been the first Silenced, and the first sent to Gaol' under

1. 97, pp. 53f., 52; R.B., III, i, §231.

the Five Miles Act of 1665, 'was the first prosecuted'[1] under this Second Conventicle Act, he observes. One wonders how he thought he knew.

On 9 June 1675 fresh warrants were sent 'to distrein on me . . . for 50 pounds'. Baxter at first kept the door locked; but eventually he sold his goods and allowed his wife to remove his books into a place of hiding, 'that I might have nothing to be distreined, and so go on to Preach'. His wife and he then left Southampton Square for Oxendon Street (off what is now Coventry Street), where his wife had taken ground on another short lease and had built 'two little houses' on the street front, as well as (with the help of £350 raised by friends whom Baxter names) a meeting-place to replace the rooms over the market-house. It was no use. Baxter 'preacht there but one day'. The Secretary of State, Henry Coventry, 'had a house joyning to it' (whence Coventry Street) and was determined 'it should not be used'. He not only 'spake twice against it, in the Parliament'[2] and caused drums to be beaten under the windows,[3] but 'got three Justices with a Warrant'[4] for Baxter's arrest on the following Sunday. When Sunday came, however, Baxter was not there.

He had been invited into the country for a period of convalescence after renewed illness by a friend of long standing, Richard Beresford, of Charleswood, Rickmansworth. Here he spent ten weeks, preaching 'often Twice a Day' at Rickmansworth, Chesham, Amersham, King's Langley and other churches in the neighbourhood. Some of these churches, the 'Invitation' to which he owed to Beresford's 'great Industry', were then in the diocese of London, for preaching in which he had Sheldon's licence of 1661 and held this to be still valid. Rickmansworth, he says, was the first parish church in which he had ventured to preach since 1662; he was not a stranger to it, for he had been there earlier, directly after the Savoy Conference. He also used Beresford's house for an apologetic purpose. Quakerism was strong at Rickmansworth, where at the time William Penn was living at Basing House. Baxter 'was desirous that the Poor People should Once hear what was to be said for their Recovery'[5] and had a seven hours' dispute with Penn,

---

1. *97*, p. 54; *R.B.*, III, i, §§270, 278, 306 and 276; and cf. §282.
2. *Ibid.*, §§304, 310 and 305; *97*, p. 56.
3. See St Martin-in-the Fields Vestry Minutes, as quoted in *Survey of London*, edited by Sir G. Gater and W. H. Godfrey, xx (1940), p. 102.
4. *97*, p. 57.   5. *R.B.*, III, i, §§312 and 314.

with whom he also exchanged letters.[1] He found Penn as gifted in sharp phrases as any other early Quaker but at least less offensive than the pair who had disturbed his sermon at Worcester twenty years earlier.

The minister who had preached at Oxendon Street on the first Sunday of Baxter's absence was an ejected clergyman from Derbyshire who happened to be in London that day. He was arrested and imprisoned in Baxter's stead and was not released for nearly three months, when Sir Matthew Hale intervened and 'proved the Mittimus void'.[2] When Baxter returned to London the justices 'were now taught to stop every Hole in the next Warrant (to which I was still as liable as ever)',[3] and for the winter of 1675–6 he desisted from preaching. Two years later his wife sub-let the meeting-house in Oxendon Street to the new Vicar of St Martin-in-the-Fields, 'and the Parishioners accepted of it for their publick Worship'.[4] But she was not yet to be beaten. In the meantime she proceeded to hire another room, still in the parish, in Swallow Street, this time a meeting-house ready built; and there on 16 April 1676 Baxter began to preach again.

Later that month his friend Joseph Read was 'taken out of the Pulpit' in the meeting-place in his own house and sent to prison; but for a time Baxter himself was not interfered with. On 9 November, however, 'six Constables, four Beadles, and many Messengers, were set at the Chappel-doors' in Swallow Street to execute a fresh warrant; and they 'continued guarding the Door of the Chappel for above Four and twenty Lord's days after'. Henceforth, though she still used her money to help in building meeting-houses, Mrs Baxter abandoned her efforts to provide one for her husband's use. Instead, 'it was her choice that I should go quite to Southwark each Lords-day', to a congregation in Globe Alley whose minister had died in November; and there Baxter 'preached many Months in peace' in 1677, 'there being no Justice willing to disturb us'.[5]

1. See R. Thomas in Friends' Historical Society *Journal*, xlviii, 5 (spring, 1958), pp. 204–7.
2. *134*, p. 38.
3. *R.B.*, III, i, §316.
4. *97*, p. 57. In 1807 the building came into the hands of a Scottish congregation of Anti-Burgher Original Seceders, and the name is still preserved in a mission of the Hampstead English Presbyterian congregation.
5. *R.B.*, III, i, §328 and ii, §4f.; *97*, p. 59.

It is a curious comment on this 'period of piebald persecution',[1] as it has been called, that interspersed with these efforts to prevent Baxter from preaching were efforts by others to engage his help in effecting better relations between Nonconformists and the Church of England. He had friends in the Church as well as foes, and friends well placed. At both Acton and Totteridge it was his custom to join regularly in Common Prayer, as we have seen. Earlier also, before he left London for Acton in 1663, he went 'ordinarily . . . to some Parish Church' with 'a Learned Minister that . . . preached well, (as Dr Wilkins, Dr Tillotson, Mr Nest, &c.)'.[2] John Wilkins, who in 1668 became Bishop of Chester, was at this time Vicar of St Lawrence Jewry; and the future Archbishop of Canterbury, John Tillotson, though not yet Tuesday Lecturer at St Lawrence's, often preached there for Wilkins. The two men became associated in a number of ways. In 1664 Tillotson married Wilkins's step-daughter; and when in 1672 (on the day that Baxter first used his licence to preach) Wilkins died, at Tillotson's house, he appointed Tillotson his executor. Wilkins had married a sister of Oliver Cromwell and Tillotson had been brought up in the Congregational church at Sowerby, Yorkshire. Both men desired a policy of moderation and concessions towards Nonconformists and were in touch with Baxter to this end. In 1668 Wilkins and Baxter, with two other Nonconformist leaders, William Bates and Thomas Manton, were engaged in conferences concerning proposals drawn up by Wilkins for the comprehension of Nonconformists within the Church. 'We came to a full Agreement, which Judge Hale, . . . greatly approving it, drew up in an Act to be offered the Commons'; but they 'Voted to receive no such Act'. In 1673 Lord Broghill, now the Earl of Orrery, requested Baxter to draw up proposals of a kind that 'would satisfie the Non-conformists so far as to unite us all against Popery; professing that he met with many Great Men that were much for it'. In 1675, once more, Baxter and Manton had meetings with Tillotson, who was now Dean of Canterbury, and with the Rector of St Andrew's, Holborn, Edward Stillingfleet, and 'came to an Agreement'; but on 11 April Tillotson wrote to Baxter, 'I do most heartily desire an Accommodation, and shall always endeavour it' but 'the Concurrence of a

1. R. Thomas, in *From Uniformity to Unity*, p. 214.
2. *R.B.*, I, ii, §433. Thomas Neast was Rector of St Martin's, Iremonger Lane.

considerable part of the Bishops, and the Countenance of his Majesty . . . at present I see little reason to expect'.[1]

In these repeated efforts for comprehension, continued despite the experiences of exclusion and arrest with which they were punctuated, Baxter had the support of his wife, who had no 'opinion against Episcopacy' and 'did not love . . . to hear Conformists talkt against as a Party' but was 'for universal love of all true Christians'. But in 1681, on 14 June, after a few weeks' illness, his wife died; and with her something in him died too. In moving words he wrote of her that 'her understanding was . . . like the treble strings of a Lute, strained up to the highest, sweet, but in continual danger'; and that 'her knife was too keen, and cut the sheath'. This was true. But it was also true that she 'was all for mildness, calmness, gentleness, pleasingness and serenity' in him and that her death removed a restraint from the 'impatient Temper of Mind' and habit of sharp speaking which Baxter admitted in himself and which she was apt bluntly to call 'over selfish queralousness'.[2] She was buried in her mother's grave in Christ Church, Newgate, then in ruins after the Great Fire of 1666.

Baxter's loss of his wife was accentuated by the fact that, as he puts it, she was 'gone after many of my choicest Friends, who within this one year are gone to Christ, and I am following even at the door'. Sir Matthew Hale had died earlier, in 1676. John Corbet, who had shared Baxter's home at Totteridge, died in December 1680; in the previous August Baxter's stepmother had died, aged ninety-six, after 'Thirty years longing to be with Christ' and 'at last rejoycing in the triumphant frequent hearing and repeating the 91. Psalm'; and in May 1681 his 'old Friend and Housekeeper' at Kidderminster, who had 'eased me of all Care, and laid out all my Money for Housekeeping, so that I never had one Hour's trouble about it'. Her place was now to be taken by a 'Grave Matron', Mrs Bushel, who became Baxter's 'Faithful Friend, and Constant Attendant'[3] and was with him at his death. This was still ten years away, but came after a gradual decay which set in when his wife died. His periodic additions to his autobiography begin to dry up, the last being written in January 1685; his handwriting grows increasingly crabbed and crotchety; and an

---

1. *R.B.*, appendix viii, p. 121; III, i, §§256 and 287.
2. *97*, pp. 48, 75, 68, 90, 73 and 78; *R.B.*, I, i, §213 *ad fin.* (p. 138).
3. *97*, epistle to reader; *R.B.*, III, ii, §67; I, i, §137 (28); M. Sylvester, *Elisha's Cry* p. 16.

inveterate habit of self-justification hitherto held in restraint now gets the better of him in too many of his published pieces.

He was not, however, to be left to grow old in peaceful melancholy. On 20 October 1682[1] 'I was (being newly risen from Extremity of pain) suddenly surprized in my house by a poor violent Informer, and many Constables and others, who rusht in and apprehended me, and served on me' six warrants 'to distrain for an Hundred and ninty pounds, for five Sermons'.

They Executed all their Warrants on my Books and Goods; even the bed that I lay sick on, and sold them all. . . . I borrowed some Bedding and Necessaries, [but] they threatned to come upon me again . . .: So that I had no remedy, but utterly to forsake my House and Goods and all, and take secret Lodgings distant in a stranger's House.[2]

Nor was this the end. Two years later, in November 1684, 'Warrants to apprehend me' arrived again. On this occasion, as once before, Baxter at first kept the door locked. 'But they set six Officers at my Study-door, who watcht all night, and kept me from my bed and food, so that the next day I yielded to them.' For the time being, the Justices contented themselves with binding him over to good behaviour, and this was renewed in December and again in January 1685, 'tho' no one ever accused me for any Conventicles or Preaching since they took all my Books and Goods above two years ago, and I for the most part keep my bed'.[3] A month later, on 28 February, he was arrested and imprisoned in the King's Bench prison in Southwark. His trial before Judge Jeffreys took place during May and June. After his death Tillotson, now Archbishop of Canterbury, wrote to Matthew Sylvester, who was to edit Baxter's autobiography, urging him to tell of the scene in Westminster Hall:

nothing more honourable than when the Rev. Baxter stood at bay, berogued, abused, despised; never more great than then. Draw this well. You will say, this will not be borne; it may, if well done; and if it will not be borne now, it will hereafter; and the time will come when it may and will be known.[4]

It has been known since 1702, when Edmund Calamy published his *Abridgment* of Sylvester's work; and since 1849, when Macaulay

1. For the date, see D.W.L., Morrice MSS., Entring Book, 1:339.
2. *R.B.*, III, ii, §76.
3. *Ibid.*, §§84 and 89.
4. D.W.L. MSS., 2:76, printed by Powicke, ii, p. 294.

spent some vivid paragraphs on the scene in his *History of England*, it has been notorious.

The pretext for Baxter's arrest was new and exceedingly curious. Since 1657, when he acceded to a friend's request that he should try his hand at a paraphrase of Romans vii, he had been interested in this form of veiled commentary; and early in 1685 he published an extended *Paraphrase on the New Testament*. It was this that brought him into fresh trouble. The pamphleteer Sir Roger L'Estrange, 'the Dog Towzer' as the mob called him when they burnt him in effigy in 1680, had long carried on intermittent warfare with Baxter in such pieces as *A Relaps'd Apostate* (1661) and *The Casuist Uncas'd* (1680), and in a news-sheet which he ran from 1681 to 1687, *The Observator*, he traduced Baxter repeatedly. Shortly after the accession of James II, on 28 February 1685, he vehemently attacked Baxter's *Paraphrase on the New Testament* as intended to incite rebellion and schism under cover of holy writ, certain passages of which, he claimed, were abused for this purpose. That the broken old man, now close on seventy, should be accused and found guilty of sedition was absurd and ridiculous; but found guilty he was, fined five hundred marks and sentenced to prison till it was paid. To Baxter himself, 'to be ragingly reviled by Jefferies and Withins, and called Rogue and Knave, and not suffered to speak one word of answer for my self and my Council reviled that offered to speak for me, was far harder than my Imprisonment'.[1]

'I went quietly,' he says, 'to a costly Prison, where I continued in pain and languor near two years';[2] and 'had not the King taken off my Fine, I had continued in Prison till death'.[3] Actually, he was not confined to the prison in Southwark, at least not for the whole period; for when Matthew Henry, son of the ejected incumbent of Worthenbury, Flintshire, visited him on 17 November 1685, he 'found him in pretty comfortable circumstances, though a prisoner, in a private house near the prison, attended on by his own man and maid'. There was an interesting flash-back to the time forty years earlier when Baxter had left Coventry to join the Parliamentarians in relieving the siege of Wem. 'He inquired for his Shropshire friends, and observed, that of those gentlemen who were

---

1. *134*, p. 40. Sir Francis Wythens's legal career is described as one of 'compliant subservience' (*Dictionary of National Biography*).
2. *Ibid.*
3. *122* (2nd ed., 1695), n. *ad fin.*

with him at Wem, he hears of none whose sons tread in their
fathers' steps but Colonel Hunt's.' The old man was a Salopian
at heart still. He did not lose the opportunity to improve the
occasion. 'He said we who are young are apt to count upon great
things, but we must not look for it.'[1] He spoke from experience
as well as from Jeremiah 45:4–5.

A year later, on 24 November 1686, his fine was remitted and he
was released from prison. He was still bound over to good behaviour
but he was granted permission to live in London. On 28 February
1687 he took a house in Charterhouse Yard (now Charterhouse
Square) in Finsbury, not far from the district where his wife and
he had lived when they first came to London and where she was
buried. It was 'the fourth door' from Rutland House, where
Matthew Sylvester, who in his youth had been ejected from a
living in Lincolnshire, lived and ministered to a congregation
meeting there. Sylvester had been acquainted with Baxter since
1671 and had accompanied him when in 1675 he went for convalescence to Rickmansworth. Baxter now joined with Sylvester, in
an honorary capacity, in what the younger man was proud to call
'Copartnership', though he says Baxter 'would stile himself (when
somewhat pleasant) my Curate'. 'He would not meddle with the
Pastoral Work';[2] but under protection of the general Declaration
of Indulgence to Nonconformists issued by James II on 11 April
1687 he could preach to this licensed congregation; and, though
'scarce able to creep once a day to our Assembly',[3] he did preach
there, when he was well enough, every Sunday morning and on
alternate Thursdays for the next four and a half years.

On 10 November 1689 a Scottish minister, Robert Kirk of
Aberfoyle, Perthshire, heard a sermon from him in this congregation from the text 'Blessed are the peacemakers'. This was the
eve of the first anniversary of James II's abdication. He wrote a
piece entitled 'King James his abdication of the crown plainly
proved'[4] only two months before his death; and on another
occasion Kirk heard him pray 'for the success of King William and

1. *Memoirs of . . . Matthew Henry*, edited by J. B. Williams (3rd ed.,
1829), p. 28f.
2. *R.B.*, Sylvester's preface to reader.
3. *134*, p. 41. The name of Rutland House is preserved in Rutland
Place, off Charterhouse Square.
4. Printed by R. Schlatter, *Richard Baxter and Puritan Politics*,
pp. 157ff.

Queen Mary in Ireland'. We may be glad that he lived into the new era ushered in by the Act of Toleration of 1689, and could dimly see some future for worship according to conscience free from ecclesiastical interference. To the last he retained his eagerness for understanding and 'comprehension'. Kirk heard him pray 'for a reconciling all differences, that party nor sect be never heard any more among Protestants';[1] and he prayed believingly. On 11 April 1691 he ended a preface to *Church Concord; . . . A Disswasive from Unnecessary Division and Separation*, a work consisting of papers written far earlier but only now published, with these words: 'the great Reconciler will in due time reconcile and closely Unite his own. Amen'.

For the last few months of 1691 he still 'open'd his Doors Morning and Evening every day to all that would come to joyn in Family-Worship with him'; till at last 'his growing Distempers and Infirmities took him also off from this, confining him first to his Chamber, and after to his Bed'.[2] The day before the end he told two friends 'I have pain, there is no arguing against sense, but I have peace, I have peace'.[3] He might have said as much on almost any day of his life for the last forty-five years; but the saints' everlasting rest was now his. He died on 8 December 1691 and was buried, as his wife had been, in Christ Church, Newgate. A theological student, who had recently joined with others in sending him an expression of unbounded admiration, in old age recalled watching the funeral procession cover the whole distance between Christ Church and its starting-point in Threadneedle Street, at the Merchant Tailors' Hall: 'streets and windows and balconies all crowded',[4] another observer wrote at the time. The funeral sermon, from Luke 23:46, was preached at Baxter's request by one of his oldest friends and companions in arms, William Bates, who published it early in 1692.

On 4 December 1924 a mural inscription was placed in the church to mark Baxter's burial there; but Christ Church, which had arisen afresh from the ruins among which Baxter's wife had been buried, was again damaged in 1941 and has now been demolished. The memorial has thus proved no more lasting than the 'very fair, rich large marble-stone' which recorded his mother-

1. Donald Maclean, *London at Worship 1689–90* (1928), p. 16.
2. M. Sylvester, *op. cit.*, p. 16.
3. W. Bates, *Funeral-Sermon for . . . R. Baxter* (1692), p. 129.
4. *Historical Manuscripts Commission, Portland*, iii, p. 485.

in-law's burial there in 1661 and which 'the fall of the Church' in 1666 broke 'all to pieces'.

But [as he wrote in his wife's memoir] Christs-Church on earth is liable to those changes of which the Jerusalem above is in no danger. . . . I hope this Paper-Monument . . . will be more publickly useful and durable than that Marble-Stone was.[1]

1. 97, p. 93f.

CHAPTER 6

A Pen in God's Hand

'God will have other Generations to succeed us: Let us thank him that we have had our time. . . .
'The Gospel dieth not when I die: The Church dieth not: The Praises of God die not; the World dieth not: And perhaps it shall grow better, and those Prayers shall be answered which seemed lost: Yea, & it may be some of the Seed that I have sowen, shall spring up to some benefit of the dark unpeaceable World when I am dead.'[1]

DURING the last thirty years of his life Baxter had been prevented from exercising pastoral oversight. His endeavours to preach, occasional though they were, had also been constantly frustrated. The one form of ministry which remained open to him was his writing. Here too he often met with opposition, both in the form of refusal to license the publication of what he had written and in the controversy, or the personal attacks, which his books when published aroused. Even so, it was among the mercies of God that

when I might not speak by Voice to any single Congregation, he enabled me to speak by Writings to many; and for the Success of my plainest & popular writings, which cost me least I can never be sufficiently thankful: Some of which he sent to preach abroad in other Languages in forreign Lands.[2]

Not that he needed the experience of involuntary inaction to stir him to write. Already at Kidderminster 'my Writings were my chiefest daily Labour'; and by 1665, when he composed the first part of his autobiography, he was able to compile a list of fifty of his books. *The Saints Everlasting Rest*, though his second book to be published, was 'the first which I began'; and 'this Book', he says, 'it pleased God so far to bless to the Profit of many, that it encouraged me to be guilty of all those Scripts which after followed'. His *Call to the Unconverted* likewise 'God hath blessed with unexpected Success beyond all the rest that I have written (except *The Saints Rest*): . . . I have had Information of almost whole Households converted by this small Book';[3] which before

1. *114*, p. 114f.   2. *Ibid.*, p. 225.
3. *R.B.*, I, i, §§135, 158 and 174.

his death had been translated into French, German, Welsh and Algonquian (the language of the American Indians).

Privately, Baxter shared his wife's opinion of his books: 'fewer well studied and polished had been better'. 'I could wish,' he writes, looking back, 'I had rather been doing some work of more durable Usefulness.' Even at the time this would have satisfied him better: 'my own Desire was rather to stay upon one thing long, than run over many'. But 'many as they are, I wrote none which I thought needless at the time of writing them'.[1] 'Some sudden Occasions or other extorted almost all my Writings from me: and the Apprehension of Present Usefulness or Necessity prevailed against all other Motives'; so that 'I scarce ever wrote one Sheet twice over, nor stayed to make any Blots or Interlinings, but was fain to let it go as it was first conceived'. Baxter's manuscripts confirm this observation. Their cleanness is remarkable; all the more so, if they were composed not at leisure but by one writing 'in the Crowd of all my other Imployments', who 'thought some considerable work still called for haste: I have these Forty years been still sensible of the sin of losing time: I could not spare an hour'.[2]

In writing his books Baxter also says he sought, or was divinely used, to return to others something of the 'helps' and 'Blessing' which books had brought to himself. He had spent 'many hundred studious Days and Weeks'; then 'the Love of Man, and the Love of Truth, oblige me to be soberly Communicative'.[3] Even in boyhood 'I prosecuted all my Studies with unweariedness and delight'.[4] Later, 'methinks I could bid the world farewel', he wrote in *The Saints Everlasting Rest*, 'and immure my self among my Books, and look forth no more (were it a lawful course)'.[5] The decade then before him in Kidderminster was filled with activity in his parish, in Worcestershire, and farther afield; and when after 1662 he entered a period of enforced seclusion, part of its bitterness lay in his now being without his 'too much beloved Library'.[6] 'I live only for Work,' he wrote in 1670 to the Duke of Lauderdale, who had offered him a choice of high positions if he would come to Scotland; and he went on to plead that 'I might live quietly to follow my private Study, and might once again have the use of my

1. *Ibid.*, §212; *71*, pt iii, p. 199.   2. *R.B.*, I, i, §212; *97*, p. 78.
3. *R.B.*, I, i, §212; *71*, pt iii, p. 199.   4. *R.B.*, I, i, §5.
5. *2*, p. 807.   6. *114*, p. 227.

Books (which I have not seen these ten Years, and pay for a Room for their standing at Kiderminster, where they are eaten with Worms and Rats)'. After returning to London in 1672 he 'paid dear for the Carriage' of his books; only to lose them when three years later his goods were distrained on as a penalty for preaching: 'so that if Books had been my Treasure (and I valued little more on Earth) I had now been without a treasure'.[1]

When in 1683 he published his *Dying Thoughts*, he did not fail to include among the divine mercies of his life that

> my Library hath afforded me both profitable and pleasant company and help at all times, when ever I would use them. I have dwelt among the shining Lights, which the Learned, Wise and Holy men of all Ages have set up, and left to illuminate the World.
> [But now] I must leave my Library, and turn over those pleasant Books no more.[2]

The overt reference here is to the death he believed to be imminent. The words take on additional poignancy when one knows that, shortly before, what books he had latterly accumulated had again been 'seized and sold', while of 'multitudes of Manuscripts that had long lain by me . . . I cast away whole Volumes; which I could not carry away'.[3]

The fact that at his death in 1691 Baxter left a library of over 1,400 books, which he bequeathed to such 'young students' as his literary executors should nominate, together with a mass of manuscripts now bound in twenty-six volumes in Dr Williams's Library,[4] need cast no doubt on his veracity. A library many times as large would be needed if room were to be made for all the books of which lists for recommended reading appear constantly throughout his writings. The longest of these lists, which contains over a thousand titles, he still provides as suitable only for 'the Poor mans Library'.[5] Some of the titles may have been culled from published catalogues; but the brief comments often added in the course of the lists leave no room for doubt of his familiarity with the contents of very many of the books mentioned.

1. *R.B.*, III, i, §§171 and 309.
2. *114*, pp. 223f. and 87.
3. *R.B.*, III, ii, §76; *114*, preface.
4. See G. F. Nuttall, 'Transcript of Richard Baxter's Library Catalogue', in *Journal of Ecclesiastical History*, II, 2 and III, 1 (October 1951 and April 1952); and *Baxter Treatises*, edited by R. Thomas.
5. *71*, pt iii, p. 194.

Much of Baxter's manuscript correspondence, also, is filled with inquiries after books or comments on them. Bibliographers have remarked not only on the speed with which he published answers to books written against him but on the promptness with which, in order to do so, he must have received these books. A work entitled *Sincerity and Hypocrisy* published in 1658 by W.S., the last chapter of which, 'by another hand', animadverts on Baxter's doctrine of grace, is dated April 1658 by the contemporary book-collector, George Thomason. Yet the dedicatory epistle of Baxter's book *Of Saving Faith*, the last chapter of which contains his retort, is dated 31 March 1658. He had in fact received a copy of *Sincerity and Hypocrisy* on 13 March.[1] He also knew, and revealed at the time, the identity both of W.S. (William Sheppard, serjeant-at-law during the Commonwealth) and of 'another hand' (Thomas Barlow, then Bodley's Librarian and later Bishop of Lincoln), and both attributions have been accepted.

For the latest news as well as the latest books Baxter found his London publishers, Thomas Underhill and Francis Tyton, a useful source. They also acted as intermediaries for correspondence through London to and from Essex or the south-west. On one occasion Tyton writes on the outside of a letter from Somerset that he has no news and therefore writes no letter, thereby saving Baxter's money.[2] The publishers also followed his directions in distributing copies of his books to his friends as a form of royalty. 'I get not a farthing to myself for any book I print,' he writes in a letter of 1657; 'the fifteenth book I have, to give my friends.'[3]

The extent and variety of his correspondence matches those of his published writings. By way of excuse for the delay in his reply to two letters from a regular correspondent, he writes in 1653: 'I could not do it till now. Necessity hath no law. I now take yours from among a dozen that have lain unanswered.'[4] A quarter of a century later, things were still the same: 'This Day while I am writing these words, my Pockets are too full of Letters sent me.'[5]

1. *Catalogue of the pamphlets . . . collected by George Thomason, 1640–1661* (British Museum, 1908), ii, p. 205; F. Madan, *Oxford Books*, iii (Oxford, 1931), p. 89, no.2412; D.W.L. MS., 1:198.

2. D.W.L. MS., 1:193.

3. *Ibid.*, 4:257; cf. *R.B.*, appendix vii and the passage printed at end of both *35* and *36*.

4. D.W.L. MS., 1:198.

5. *114*, p. 104.

More than a thousand letters are still preserved at Dr Williams's Library and elsewhere.[1] Most of these are letters received by Baxter, but he also kept copies of many of his own letters, especially those dealing with theological issues. Something of the range of his correspondence over the Voluntary Associations of ministers which sprang up all over England during the Commonwealth and Protectorate has appeared in an earlier chapter. Controversy over the nature of grace; the authorship of the Apostles' creed; the antiquity of the observance of Christmas; the right subjects for the reception of baptism and the Lord's Supper; plans for raising money to send poor students to the university; the duties of a chaplain at Cromwell's court or of a newly elected Member of Parliament: on these and a multitude of other weighty topics Baxter was always ready with his opinion and advice. He was no less generous when his help was sought by an adolescent oppressed by the desire to masturbate or by a middle-aged woman troubled with melancholia.

Throughout his correspondence, however, no topic recurs so frequently as that of books—the best books on a subject; or the latest book—and over and over again his correspondents write to thank him for his own books. They often use their admiration as a means of introducing themselves to him. 'All books that I know extant of yours I have,' writes William White, Rector of Pusey, Berkshire, in 1654, 'and most of 'em have read through (giving God hearty thanks for the light and guidance that he hath afforded me by and in them).' 'Be assured,' writes Henry Bartlett, Vicar of Fordingbridge, Hampshire, in 1655, 'you are high in our affections, frequent in our prayers, and your *Rest* and *Directions* next to the Bible the choice books among us all.' Three days later the Rector of Newington Butts, Surrey, Thomas Wadsworth, writes expressing his admiration for the 'crystalline perspicuity' of Baxter's *Aphorismes* and the 'heavenliness' of *The Saints Everlasting Rest*, adding, 'I value them above all the books I have, or ever (I had almost said) hope to see.' In 1657 the Earl of Lauderdale wrote from Windsor Castle, where he was in prison, 'I have reason to esteem' *The Saints Everlasting Rest* 'above all books except the Bible'; and in 1658 Thomas Gouldstone, Rector of Finchley, Middlesex, 'my second birth, if yet born again, I owe to you, you

1. cf. G. F. Nuttall, 'Richard Baxter's Correspondence: a Preliminary Survey', in *Journal of Ecclesiastical History*, I, 1 (April 1950).

are my father, your *Saints Rest* I mean, which I read three times over in the year 51'.[1]

Other letters express their writers' disapproval of Baxter's books, or of passages in them. It was an age of inspissated controversy. When in 1665 Baxter inserted in his autobiography the titles and occasions of the fifty books he had then written, he also recorded that 'there are about Fifty Books (as I remember) that in whole or in part are written against me', some of them, as he puts it elsewhere, 'adorned with the flowers of Billingsgate Rhetorick'.[2] None of his books aroused more criticism than his first, *Aphorismes of Justification* (1649), on account of which, almost as soon as it was out of the press, he described himself to a neighbour as 'hissed at' by 'most divines'.[3] Four years later he writes that he has 'utterly suppressed ... that offensive book, against the importunity of forty letters'.[4] This did not prevent its reappearance 'surreptitiously printed ... against my will'.[5]

In 1665 Baxter writes: 'In my youth I was quickly ... running up into a multitude of Controversies ...: But the elder I grew the smaller stress I layd upon these Controversies and Curiosities.'[6] His later practice, it is true, hardly bears this out: the pieces he published during the 1680s are predominantly controversial; partly, no doubt, because this was a period in which the frustration he met with on all hands became increasingly hard to bear. Yet it is fair to remember his willingness to retract and revoke when convinced of error. In a book published in 1709, written to correct what the author believed to be a mistaken judgement of Baxter's, a minister twenty-five years his junior wrote of him that 'not long before his Death, in private Discourse, he did seriously profess his Desires to me, that if I observed any dangerous Error in any of his Writings, in case the Lord should continue my Life after this, I would refute that Error'.[7] In the last year of his life, moreover, the old man published *Richard Baxters Penitent Confession*, in which (not without some continuing self-justification) he set out the many mistakes in his actions and writings which he now perceived and regretted.

1. D.W.L. MSS., 5:225, 6:112, 2:250, 4:104, 5:121; by *Directions* is meant Baxter's *Right Method for a Settled Peace of Conscience* (1653); 'crystalline' is charmingly spelt 'Christaline'.
2. *R.B.*, I, i, §155; *8*, pt iv, 2nd postscript.
3. D.W.L. MS., 3:253; printed in *3* (3rd edition), p. 409.
4. D.W.L. MS., 1:11.   5. *R.B.*, I, i, §163.   6. *Ibid.*, §213 (3).
7. Increase Mather, *Dissertation Concerning the Future Conversion of the Jewish Nation* (1709), p. 2.

Nor was this a sign of any senile weakening of nerve. In 1665 he had already allowed 'by way of penitent Confession, that I am too much inclined to such words in Controversal Writings which are too keen, and apt to provoke the Person whom I write against', and had added, 'I repent of it, and wish all over-sharp passages expunged from my Writings, and desire forgiveness of God and Man.'[1]

When in 1653 he published *The Right Method for a Settled Peace of Conscience*, the Master of Trinity College, Cambridge, Thomas Hill, wrote that it 'displeases many, about perseverance left so uncertain'; and the Rector of Donhead St Mary, Wiltshire, Peter Ince, wrote likewise that 'many good men were very much troubled at your opinion, that it is so staggering about perseverance'.[2] Baxter's reply to Ince is so revealing that it is worth reproducing with many omissions but still at some length.

My strong opinion is for perseverance: I hope that's no error: if I hold not the truth by such a full certainty as others, must I therefore be an Arminian? my intellect is not at the command of my will! nor of the will of my friends! only evidence forceth it, and I hope the spirit of truth doth guide it.

While we close in Christ and hold him fast in love and obedience, I scarce mind these pettish exceptions. I have in some measure learned to love a Christian merely as a Christian, and to hear all the chidings of dissenters but as the unavoidable effects of our childish infirmities. It hath cost me three or four years' labours mainly, to write private replies to the animadversions of many brethren, nor is it a very easy labour to me to sit writing most nights till nine o'clock to the ruin of my little health, and all to satisfy the offended!

I must tell you, I am more faulty in being too tenacious of my opinions (I think) than in being too mutable. I am as unapt to give up my understanding to any man, and to go upon trust, as most men that ever yet I was acquainted with; and do suspect rather that my fault lies that way. I am more firmly established against Arminianism than ever I was in my life: above all, methinks my prayers confute it.

Nor will I lie and make myself wiser than I am to be thought orthodox. I have oft marvelled at men's strangeness to their own common ignorance in an utterly unsearchable thing: if I cannot be accounted orthodox till my ignorance in this be cured, farewell that reputation of orthodoxness in this life.[3]

There is much here that is highly characteristic; and nothing more so than the combination of honesty and earnestness. Baxter

---

1. *R.B.*, I, i, §213 (2).   2. D.W.L. MSS., 5:237 and 1:10.
3. *Ibid.*, 1:11.

never tired of insisting on what he held to be the due claims of reason, or the intellect, and on the necessity for man to be swayed not by prejudice, fashion or convention, but by evidence, if in the search for truth he were to be truly human and thus to honour God who created him man.

The Spirit of God supposeth Nature, and worketh on Man as Man; by exciting your own Understanding and Will to do their parts.
The Spirit worketh not on the Will but by the Reason; He moveth not a man as a beast or stone, to do a thing he knoweth not why; but by illumination giveth him the soundest Reason for the doing of it.
He works on man as man, and causeth him to believe nothing but what is credible.
Where is it that the Spirit giveth light, but into our own Understandings? And how perceive we that light, but by the rational apprehensions and discourses of those Understandings?[1]

One implication of this position, as appears in Baxter's reply to Peter Ince, is that in some matters it is only honest to confess to agnosticism; another, that it is necessary to abandon any desire to be accounted orthodox, or any fear of being charged with heresy, in the ready but superficial manner common at certain levels of discussion. During his life Baxter was charged now with being a Papist, now an Arminian, now a Socinian; till in 1681, in comment on a book newly published, he wrote, 'the Author knoweth not what to call me, unless it be a Baxterian, as intending to be a *Haeresiarcha*'. He added: 'If you know not, I will tell you, I am a CHRISTIAN, a MEER CHRISTIAN. . . . If the Name CHRISTIAN be not enough, call me a CATHOLICK CHRISTIAN.'[2] 'Orthodoxness,' he wrote in his *Apology* (1654), 'is one of the deluders of hypocrites'; but he also, and in the same work, wrote, 'If you can make me believe that the Papists are as orthodox as you pretend them to be, you will but exceedingly glad my heart, and not a whit remove me from my own opinion.'[3] 'I am no Arminian,' he says elsewhere; but also, with reference to the Calvinist doctrine of divine predestination to sin and damnation, 'May not all common Christians well take up with a contented ignorance here?'[4] So again, 'In some mens mouths, Socinianisme is but a word of reproach, or a stone to throw at the head of any man that saith not as they. . . . But I had rather study what is Scripture-truth, then what is Socinianisme.'[5] 'Shall men be

1. *71*, pt ii, pp. 76 and 99; *14*, preface, fol. d4 and 1st pag., p. 104.
2. *91*, preface, fols. a4, b1.
3. *8*, pt iii, epistle dedicatory and pt iv., p. 12.
4. *2* (1652 edition), 2nd pag., p.38 margin.   5. *1*, p. 306.

judged Socinians for advancing the Scriptures as the only Rule?'[1]

With this position the following comment on the history of the Church will be seen to be consonant. 'Two things,' Baxter writes, 'have set the Church on fire, and been the plagues of it above one thousand years. 1. Enlarging our Creed, and making more fundamentals than ever God made. 2. Composing (and so imposing) our Creeds and Confessions in our own words and phrases.' 'O what mischief hath the Church of Christ suffered by the enlarging of her Creed! . . . Every new Article that was added to the Creed, was a new engine to stretch the brains of believers, and in the issue to rend out the bowels of the Church.'[2] When in 1654 Baxter was summoned to London to assist in the conference called to decide in what terms 'the Fundamentals of Religion' essential to Christian faith should be phrased, he expressed his conviction in this matter in a way which at once roused opposition from the more orthodox as dangerous minimising. For he pleaded that the Apostles' 'Creed, Lord's Prayer, and Decalogue alone' should be offered 'as our Essentials or Fundamentals'; and when other commissioners complained, 'A Socinian or a Papist will Subscribe all this, I answered them, So much the better.'[3] It is no wonder that he was misunderstood; or that his desire for Christian unity was ineffective, then and always.

Yet from this position he never wavered. In liturgical usage he opposed any reintroduction of ceremonies not 'mere circumstances' but 'primarily doctrinal, symbolical or sacramental'. 'Scripture sufficiency and the nullity of any such universal sovereignty,' as pope or general council 'are in my judgement,' he insisted, 'the two legs of our whole reformation.'[4] In doctrine, equally, he steadily opposed the adoption as a necessary term of Christian communion of more than adherence to the Bible and the Apostles' Creed. 'The Reasons, why I make no larger a Profession necessary . . . are, because if we depart from this old sufficient Catholick Rule, we narrow the Church, and depart from the old Catholicism: . . . We shall never have done with the Papists, if we let go the Scripture-Sufficiency.' This was in 1669, in correspondence with John Owen, who urged acceptance of 'the Creed, as expounded in the Four

1. *2* (1652 edition), pt ii, preface, fol. R7 verso margin.
2. *Ibid.*, *loc. cit.* and p. 523.
3. R.B., I, ii, §52.
4. D.W.L. MS., 1:129.

first Councils', in order to exclude Socinians. 'I can readily sub-scribe my self,' Baxter added, 'but it's better let them all alone, and not to be so fond of one only Engine, which hath torn the Church for about 1200 Years.'[1]

In a too little known study cf 'Baxter as a Founder of Liberal Nonconformity', Alexander Gordon writes:

His sense of the homage due from theology to reason vindicates for Baxter a position of the first moment among the Christian teachers of his time. He is a pioneer in that whole class of studies whose object is to elucidate and demonstrate the reasonableness of Christianity, the pre-cursor of Locke in this respect, as in some others.

Locke's *Reasonableness of Christianity as delivered in the Scriptures* (1695) owes more than its title to Baxter's *Reasons for the Christian Religion* (1667).[2]

These observations come from a Unitarian scholar of an earlier generation in the course of a brief history of Unitarianism in this country. It may seem strange that Baxter should be claimed as a founding-father by the section of Dissent which in time came to hold the Arminian, Arian and Socinian tenets which he explicitly repudiated. Ironical it may be, but it is none the less justifiable historically, so far. Those who in 1719 declined to subscribe to the doctrine of the Trinity did not fail to refer to Baxter's desire for terms of communion wide enough to admit a Socinian. Through-out the eighteenth century, moreover, whenever the issue of doctrinal subscription was raised, appeal was made to the principle of Scripture-sufficiency. In an age of apologetic controlled by canons for the interpretation of Scripture other than Baxter's, application of the principle might naturally lead far from the faith as Baxter held it. This did not in itself make it improper to recall his insistence on the principle.

In the growth in England of a Unitarianism marked by what Gordon calls its 'freedom from prepossession', one of the great names is that of Joseph Priestley, of whom Gordon says elsewhere that 'the history of his religious mind exhibits a continuous renunciation of prepossessions'.[3] Here also it is fair to trace the

---

1. *R.B.*, III, i, §142 f.
2. A. Gordon, *Heads of English Unitarian History*, pp. 99 and 31f. Baxter also published works entitled *More Reasons for the Christian Religion* and, earlier, *The Unreasonableness of Infidelity* (1655).
3. A. Gordon, *op. cit.*, p. 39; *Dictionary of National Biography*, *s.v.* Priestley.

influence on Priestley of Baxter's refusal 'to go upon trust', 'on the
credit of man'.[1] Again, in his endeavours after a genuinely historical treatment of Scripture which went beyond, and behind,
patristic interpretation, Priestley was likewise only expanding, if in
a fresh manner, Baxter's principle of Scripture-sufficiency. Baxter
was well acquainted with the Fathers and refers constantly to them
throughout his writings. He knew them well enough to say that
they 'never unanimously consented in any exposition of the greatest
part of the Scriptures at all'. 'Many of them are very weak and dry.
The chief use of the Fathers is to know Historically what Doctrine
was then taught.'[2]

Yet all this represents only one side of Baxter's teaching and
personality. By itself it would not be far from falsification.

An Historical belief which is true in its kind . . . you may come to by
Rational perswasions, without special Grace: But not that deep and
firm Belief, which shall carry over the will effectually to God in Christ,
and captivate the whole man into the obedience of his will.

The Spirit and Reason are not to be here dis-joyned, much less
opposed; . . . Reason sufficeth not without the spirit, being dark and
asleep.

He that hath both the Spirit of Sanctification, and acquired Gifts of
Knowledge together, is the Compleat Christian, and likely to know
much more, then he that hath either of these alone.[3]

The fact is that, while Baxter gives reason what he believes to be
its due place, he never gives it primacy. Divine grace, inspiration,
sanctification must also receive their due place. Alongside his
strenuous defence of rationality is a quivering sensitiveness to the
world of faith: an overpowering sense of God's presence; constantly renewed gratitude for God's mercies and response to God's
demand for serious holiness; and a controlling assurance of life
beyond death and of things not seen but eternal. 'The Love of the
end is it that is the poise or spring, which setteth every Wheel a
going, and must put us on to all the means: [and] a Man is no more
a Christian indeed than he is Heavenly.'[4] At the end of his long
work on *The Reasons of the Christian Religion* Baxter suddenly cries,
as if he were weary with forbearing and could not stay, 'Thy
presence makes a croud, a Church; thy converse maketh a closet,

1. D.W.L. MS., 1:11; *8*, pt iv, p. 12.
2. *71*, pt i, p. 115, and pt iii, p. 199.
3. *14*, preface, fol. d1 and 2nd pag., p. 157; *71*, pt ii, p. 99.
4. *R.B.*, I, i, §213 (8).

or solitary wood or field, to be kin to the Angelical Chore.'[1] So, in his *Dying Thoughts*, he prays:

> My Lord, I know that Heaven is not far from me! . . . Is not Faith a seeing Grace? . . . It is not Heaven on Earth that I am begging for, But that I may see it from Mount Nebo, and have the bunch of Grapes; the Pledge, and the first-Fruits; that Faith and Hope which may kindle Love and Desire, and make me run my Race in Patience, and live, and die in the Joy which beseemeth an Heir of Heaven![2]

This element in Baxter's piety has always impressed those who have read him, whether or not they have allowed themselves to come under its power. It can hardly have failed to make itself felt in the quotations from his writings throughout this book. It pervades his personality and his reader can never forget it for long. But its impact is more effectual if it is left oblique and cumulative. To seek to present it in argumentative form, with further quotations, would be out of place. The relation of faith and reason, however, is at any time a matter of delicacy. To observe what for Baxter was their point of intersection may be illuminating.

Throughout his life Baxter was keenly interested in the occult. Almost the last of his books, the postscript to which was written less than four months before his death, *The Certainty of the Worlds of Spirits*, has as its running head 'An Historical Discourse of Apparitions and Witches'. It is an absorbing collection. Its contents pass from 'The Devil of Mascon' and 'The Witches hanged in Suffolk and Essex', through 'Mr Farmworth of an Indian Sacrifice to the Devil', 'Knockers and Death-Lights' and 'the Oundle-Well', to 'good Angels, and some doubtful Spirits' and 'the Glastonbury-Thorn'. Some of it comes from earlier collections; but in compiling it Baxter ransacked the correspondence of a life-time, and the many contemporary stories are duly attested with signatures, dates and places.

From this book a patient and well-informed student can recover otherwise unknown details about many of Baxter's acquaintances, from his old friend the Earl of Orrery to Daniel Williams, in whose library his manuscripts now lie; but in the preface Baxter warns the reader that he wrote the book 'not to please Men with the Strangeness and Novelty of useless Stories' but 'for Practice': as 'confirming helps', by their 'Evidence of Verity' constituting 'a

1. *57*, p. 458.
2. *114*, p. 187f.

firm Foundation, and rooting' for 'Faith of Supernatural Revelation'. 'It is certain, that sometimes God still worketh Miracles,'
Baxter writes elsewhere; 'but arbitrarily and rarely, which may not
put any individual person in expectation of them.'[1] As for himself,
he can say, 'I have been and am as backward to ungrounded
credulity about wonders as most men.'[2] Nevertheless,

> Dost thou not see as great Works as these Miracles [in Scripture]
> every day and hour before thine eyes? Is it not as great a work for the
> Sun to move, as to stand still, to move 1038442. miles an hour, being
> 166 times bigger than all the Earth?[3]

The precision of these figures is a reminder that Baxter had a
modern man's proper pride in his modernity.

> Guns and Printing are but lately found out. . . . Gilberts magnetical
> discoveries, . . . the nature of many Minerals and Plants, the chief
> operations and effects of Chymistry . . . are all of very late invention. . . .
> Ocular demonstrations by the Telescope, and sensible experiments, are
> daily multiplyed.[4]

To Baxter's mind the evidence for witchcraft was of the same
nature as that for these recent discoveries: 'experimental', and
confirmed by the character of the age. 'I have had many convincing proofs of Witches,'[5] he says ingenuously; but it was not
his way to ask the reader to accept his *ipse dixit*.

> If any should doubt whether there be any such witches [he writes in
> *The Saints Everlasting Rest*], let him go but into Suffolk or Essex, or
> Lancashire &c. and he may quickly be informed. Sure it were strange,
> if in an age of so much knowledge and conscience, there should so many
> score of poor creatures be put to death as Witches, if it were not clearly
> manifest that they were such. . . . Hunderds are discovered in one shire.[6]

The evidence for apparitions was equally indubitable. Baxter
presented it with great care, especially the 'famous' case in 1655,
'past contradiction', to which he refers in a number of places, of

1. *71*, pt iii, p. 186.
2. *57*, p. 353.
3. *2* (1652 ed.), pt ii, preface, fol. P8 verso.
4. *57*, p. 350f.
5. *114*, p. 45.
6. *2* (1652 ed.), 1st pag., pp. 278 and 277 margin. For the large number
of witches hanged in Suffolk and Essex in 1644–6, cf. *Dictionary of
National Biography*, s.v. Matthew Hopkins.

the 'Apparition in the shape of Collonel Bowen in Glamorganshire, to his Wife and Family, speaking, walking before them, laying hold on them, hurting them in time of Prayer (the man himself then living from his Wife in Ireland).'[1] In *The Certainty of the Worlds of Spirits* he devotes fourteen pages to the evidence for the truth of this story provided in letters written at the time by ministers and other 'Credible Persons'. Writing in 1691, he adds that locally 'the Belief of the Fact . . . is as fully believed . . . as ever'.[2] If he did not believe it to be fact he would not record it. His interest in the story and his motive for recounting it so long afterwards could scarcely be better expressed than in this sentence from a letter to a friend at the time: 'I am glad L. Colonel Bowen believes there are witches, for then sure he believes there is a God, and angels, devils, or some spirits.'[3]

In his argumentative writings no less than in his devotional, that is to say, Baxter wrote (in Philip Doddridge's phrase) 'as ever in the views of eternity'.[4] It is the same with his controversial writings. In his autobiography he recalls how 'about the Day that' his book *The Church told of Mr Ed[ward] Bagshaws Scandals* 'came out, Mr Bagshaw died . . .; which made it grievous to me to think that I must write against the Dead. While we wrangle here in the dark, we are dying and passing to the World that will decide all our Controversies.'[5] It is the same with his references to his studies. Even the lack of a university education would be made up in heaven.

If Lipsius thought when he did but read Seneca, that he was even upon Olympus top, above mortality and humane things: What a case shall I be in when I am beholding Christ? . . . In one hour shall I see all difficulties vanish; and all my doubts in Physicks, Metaphysicks, Politicks, Medicine, &c. shall be resolved; so happy are the Students of that University! . . . There Commenius attempt is perfected; and all the Sciences reduced to one.[6]

Nor would only his intellectual cravings be satisfied. 'As for my Friends, they are not lost.'[7] What comfort 'to consider, that I shall

1. *57*, p. 148f.
2. *135*, p. 21.
3. D.W.L. MS., 1:129.
4. P. Doddridge, *Works*, edited by E. Williams and E. Parsons (1802–5), v, p. 431. For Baxter's influence on Doddridge, cf. G. F. Nuttall, *Richard Baxter and Philip Doddridge: a Study in a Tradition* (1951).
5. *R.B.*, III, i, §195.
6. *2*, p. 807f.   7. *98*, p. 55.

follow all those holy persons, whom I once conversed with, that are gone before me, and that I shall dwell with such as Henoch and Elias, and Abraham and Moses and Job and David, and Peter and John and Paul and Timothy . . .'. The catalogue continues through the Fathers to 'Bernard, and Gerson, and Savonarola and Mirandula, and Taulerus and Kempisius' and on through the sixteenth-century Reformers of the Continent and of this country (including Calvin, but not Luther), till he reaches contemporaries he had admired, some of them his own friends: 'Ussher and Hall, and Gataker and Bradshaw, and Vines and Ash, and millions more of the family of God.'[1] As evidence that his books meant everything to him, still more as evidence that (in three words) 'Heaven is real',[2] this list, which runs to sixty-two names, is as characteristic as it is remarkable. In its catching into one not merely earth and heaven but past, present and future there is a quality at once ingenuous and audacious which one can only call Dantesque. His friends and contemporaries recognised this. Bates puts it as simply as it can be put in his funeral sermon: 'Mr Baxter was conversant in the invisible world.'[3]

One who thus inhabits another world commonly receives from his fellow human beings a certain unwilling admiration, so long as he stays there. This is what Baxter would not do. He returned from the mountain of God to deliver men and to bring them up unto a good land and a large. His blend of faith and reason was his own and was the issue of his integrity; but its shaping as well as its manner owed everything to his desire to persuade others at once to bow to the truth and to find peace and joy in believing. His tense is commonly the imperative. He would not leave others alone; and this they resented. The man who has been in hell, or in heaven, and comes back, is an offence. Things visible and invisible are disparate, and must be kept so.

There is evidence that Baxter understood this all too human ground for the opposition he so commonly met with, and that he strove to forestall it. To the long list of those to whose company in heaven he so eagerly looked forward he adds this disarming marginal note: 'Reader, bear with this mixture: for God will own his Image when pievish contenders do deny it, or blaspheme it;

1. *71*, pt ii, p. 143. Baxter includes Luther in other similar lists.
2. *Ibid.*, p. 134.
3. W. Bates, *Funeral-Sermon for . . . Richard Baxter*, epistle dedicatory.

and will receive those whom faction and proud domination would cast out, and vilifie with scorn and slanders.' 'Mixture' was, in fact, what he insisted on offering in one sphere after another. In action, his desire for tolerance and Christian unity led him to astonish men by going both to the parish church and to 'the privater Minister and Worship' where he lived, 'yea, tho it were to one that is against Infant-Baptism by mistake'; and to wish to go 'sometimes to such as had a Liturgie as faulty as that of the Greek or Ethiopian Churches; to shew by my practice, what communion my heart hath with them all'.[1] So, in writing, his independence of judgement and his wish to acknowledge elements of truth in opposing factions made him eclectic, fond of a middle way which satisfied no one. From a position reasoned, balanced and central, which is always his own, he quickly sees and persuasively delineates the weaknesses as well as the strengths in every partial, or party, position. Contemporary readers often welcomed the exposure of others' weaknesses. As they read on they too often found his penetrating, discriminating gaze turned with merciless impartiality on themselves. In 1658 Baxter wrote to a friendly but critical correspondent: 'How can the most ductile man please God in such a world? You draw one way and he the other: what shall I do? even please God as near as I can whoever be displeased.'[2] Twenty-three years later he was in no better case. 'He is like one that will go one step on one side the Hedge, and another on the other side to avoid Uniformity,' men complained. He replied:

I earnestly desire to see that Wall or Hedge pull'd down, that Christs Flock among us may be one: ... Your thorn-hedge hath enclosed but one corner of Christs Vineyard, and I have business in the rest.
I will go sometime on both sides the Hedge, though by so doing I be scratcht.[3]

Inexhaustibly interested in every question, he sought always to be comprehensive. This appears in the very voluminousness of his writings. Their number varies with the method of computation: a single tract may be found with variant title-pages or in more than one collection, and Baxter sometimes issued part of a volume on its own account before publishing the whole. The latest of his bibliographers brings the total of works appearing before Baxter's

1. *118*, pt iv, p. 11; *71*, pt iii, p. 67.
2. D.W.L. MS., 1:198.
3. *103*, 2nd pag., pp. 84ff.

death to 133.[1] In the present study quotation is made from fewer than fifty of these, though many others have been mentioned.

This voluminousness makes Baxter in one sense elusive. One can never be altogether sure of him. There is, certainly, a marked consistency in his thought and its expression. He formed his opinions early and rarely changed them substantially. The same, or similar, phrases are to be found scattered through writings composed over a long period of years. Yet the consistency is easier to sense than to define. It comes from the character of the whole man, not merely from his intellect. It can thus yield a strangely exciting illusion of that lively power to anticipate you, and to take the initiative, which living people have, and which distinguishes life from dreams and from most books. Baxter's style is direct, penetrating and sure; yet Bates was right in saying that there is 'a noble Negligence'[2] in it.

The almost conversational manner into which he often falls, by no means only when introducing an autobiographical touch, can be very winning. Yet he wrote, it must be repeated, not to arouse interest in himself but to persuade the reader of the truth and to urge him to repent and believe the gospel. Here, both his fullness and his determination to 'drive all home'[3] are powerful in their effect. He writes, wherever he can, from his heart because 'the Transcript of the Heart hath the greatest force on the Hearts of others'.[4] But he convinces your mind also: first by forestalling the objections to his argument which were forming in it; and then by adding other objections which you had not thought of and answering these also for good measure. This copiousness sweeps you away; and just as you are happily abandoning yourself to admiration at his versatility and acuity, he draws up short; and with a simple directness that sounds as if he were there beside you, speaking to you and nobody else, understanding your condition but still respecting you, respecting you but still determined to persuade you, he forces you to forget the intellectual virtuosity and face the argument. Few writers of any age are so forceful in the suggestion that, unless you make some effective response, you are lacking in manners and also unworthy of yourself.

1. See appendix, where two items erroneously attributed to Baxter in the list followed swell the total to 135.
2. W. Bates, *op. cit.*, p. 90.
3. *17*, p. 19.
4. *R.B.*, I, i, §157.

In his last illness Baxter said to a friend: 'I was but a Pen in God's hand, and what praise is due to a Pen?'[1] To the modern mind the claim in the words is as startling as the modesty. In Baxter it is, once again, precisely the combination, the 'mixture', that is characteristic. Nor was the expression he used inadvertent, or the thought behind it new. Some years before his death he wrote:

My Lord, I have nothing to do in this World, but to seek and serve thee; I have nothing to do with a Heart and its affections, but to breathe after thee; I have nothing to do with my Tongue and Pen, but to speak to thee, and for thee, and to publish thy Glory, and thy Will.[2]

1. W. Bates, *op. cit.*, p. 125.
2. *114*, p. 214.

The Works of Richard Baxter

This list follows *The Works of Richard Baxter: an Annotated List*, compiled by A. G. Matthews [1932], revised from Congregational Historical Society *Transactions*, XI (1932).

1. *Aphorismes of Justification* (1649).
2. *The Saints Everlasting Rest* (1650).
3. *Plain Scripture Proof of Infants Church-Membership and Baptism* (1651).
4. *The Humble Petition of many thousands of the county of Worcester* (1652).
5. *The Worcester-shire Petition Defended* (1653).
6. *The Right Method for a Settled peace of Conscience* (1653).
7. *Christian Concord: or the Agreement of the Associated Pastors and Churches of Worcestershire* (1653).
8. *Richard Baxter's Apology* (1654).
9. *True Christianity* (1655).
10. *Making light of Christ and Salvation* (1655).
11. *A Sermon of Judgment* (1655).
12. *Richard Baxter's Confession of his Faith* (1655).
13. *Humble Advice* (1655).
14. *The Unreasonableness of Infidelity* (1655).
15. *The Quakers Catechism* (1655).
16. *The Agreement of divers Ministers of Christ in the county of Worcester for catechizing* (1655).
17. *Gildas Salvianus: the Reformed Pastor* (1656). Abridged edition by J. T. Wilkinson (1939).
18. *Certain Disputations of Right to Sacraments* (1657).
19. *The Safe Religion* (1657).
20. *A Treatise of Conversion* (1657).
21. *One Sheet against the Quakers* (1657).
22. *A Winding Sheet for Popery* (1657).
23. *One Sheet for the Ministry* (1657).
24. *A Second Sheet for the Ministry* (1657).

59. *The Cure of Church-Divisions* (1670).
60. *A Defence of the Principles of Love* (1671).
61. *A Second Admonition to Mr Edward Bagshaw* (1671).
62. *The Divine Appointment of the Lord's Day* (1671).
63. *The Duty of Heavenly Meditation* (1671).
64. *How far Holiness is the Design of Christianity* (1671).
65. *The Difference between the Power of Magistrates and Church-Pastors* (1671).
66. *Gods Goodness Vindicated* (1671).
67. *The Church told of Mr Ed. Bagshaw's Scandals* (1672).
68. *More Reasons for the Christian Religion* (1672).
69. *Sacrilegious Desertion of the Holy Ministry Rebuked* (1672).
70. *The Certainty of Christianity without Popery* (1672).
71. *A Christian Directory* (1673).
72. *Full and easie Satisfaction which is the true and safe Religion* (1674).
73. *The Poor Man's Family Book* (1674).
74. *An Appeal to the Light* (1674).
75. *Richard Baxter's Catholick Theologie* (1675).
76. *Two Disputations of Original Sin* (1675).
77. *More Proofs of Infants Church-Membership* (1675).
78. *Select Arguments and Reasons against Popery* (1675).
79. *A Treatise of Justifying Righteousness* (1676).
80. *Rich. Baxter's Review of the State of Christians Infants* (1676).
81. *The Judgment of Non-Conformists, of the Interest of Reason, in Matters of Religion* (1676). (Anon.)
82. *The Judgment of Nonconformists about the Difference between Grace and Morality* (1676).
83. *Roman Tradition examined* (1676). (Anon.)
84. *Naked Popery* (1677).
85. *Which is the True Church?* (1679).
86. *The Nonconformists Plea for Peace* (1679).
87. *The Second Part of the Nonconformists Plea for Peace* (1680).
88. *Richard Baxters Answer to Dr Edward Stillingfleet's Charge of Separation* (1680).
89. *The Defence of the Nonconformists Plea for Peace* (1680).
90. *A Moral Prognostication* (1680).
91. *Church-History of the Government of Bishops and their Councils abbreviated* (1680).
92. *The True and Only Way of Concord* (1680).

93. *Fasciculus literarum* (1680).
    This entry is erroneous, as Matthews later observed. The work was issued by John Hinckley. The entry is included here in order to preserve the consecutive enumeration.
94. *A True Believer's Choice and Pleasure* (1680).
95. *Faithful Souls shall be with Christ* (1681).
96. *Compassionate Counsel to all Young-Men* (1681).
97. *A Breviate of the Life of Margaret Baxter* (1681). Abridged edition by J. T. Wilkinson (1928).
98. *Poetical Fragments* (1681).
99. *An Apology for the Nonconformists Ministry* (1681).
100. *A Treatise of Episcopacy* (1681).
101. *A Second True Defence of the Meer Nonconformists* (1681).
102. *A Search for the English Schismatick* (1681).
103. *A Third Defence of the Cause of Peace* (1681).
104. *Methodus Theologiae Christianae* (1681).
105. *A Sermon preached at the funeral of John Corbet* (1681).
106. *The True History of Councils enlarged* (1682).
107. *An Answer to Mr Dodwell and Dr Sherlocke* (1682).
108. *How to Do Good to Many* (1682).
109. *Of the Immortality of Mans Soul* (1682).
110. *Additional Notes on the Life and Death of Sir Matthew Hale* (1682).
111. *The Catechizing of Families* (1683).
112. *Obedient Patience* (1683).
113. *Preparation for Sufferings* (1683).
     This entry is probably erroneous, as Matthews later observed.
114. *Richard Baxter's Dying Thoughts* (1683).
115. *Richard Baxter's Farewel Sermon* (1683).
116. *Catholick Communion Defended* (1684).
117. *Schism Detected in both Extreams* (1684).
118. *Catholick Communion Defended against both Extreams* (1684).
119. *Whether Parish Congregations be True Christian Churches* (1684).
120. *Catholick Communion Doubly Defended* (1684).
121. *The One Thing Necessary* (1685).
122. *A Paraphrase on the New Testament* (1685).
123. *R. Baxter's Sence of the Subscribed Articles of Religion* (1689).
124. *A Treatise of Knowledge and Love Compared* (1689).
125. *Cain and Abel Malignity* (1689).

126. *The Scripture Gospel Defended* (1690).
127. *The English Nonconformity* (1690).
128. *An End of Doctrinal Controversies* (1691).
129. *The Glorious Kingdom of Christ* (1691).
130. *A Reply to Mr Tho. Beverley's Answer* (1691).
131. *Of National Churches* (1691).
132. *Against the Revolt to a Foreign Jurisdiction* (1691).
133. *Church Concord* (1691).
134. *Richard Baxter's Penitent Confession* (1691).
135. *The Certainty of the Worlds of Spirits* (1691).

Posthumous:
136. *The Protestant Religion truely stated* (1692), edited by D. Williams and M. Sylvester.
137. *The Grand Question resolved* (1692).
138. *Mr Richard Baxter's Paraphrase on the Psalms* (1692), edited by M. Sylvester.
139. *Universal Redemption* (1694), edited by J. Reade and M. Sylvester.
140. *Reliquiae Baxterianae* (1696), edited by M. Sylvester. Abridged edition by J. M. Lloyd Thomas, [1925].
141. *The Poor Husbandman's Advocate* (Manchester, 1926), edited by F. J. Powicke.

Many though very far from all the above were reprinted in Baxter's *Practical Works*, 4 vols. (1707); 23 vols. (1830); 4 vols. (1868).

Index